The
Fabric
Decorator

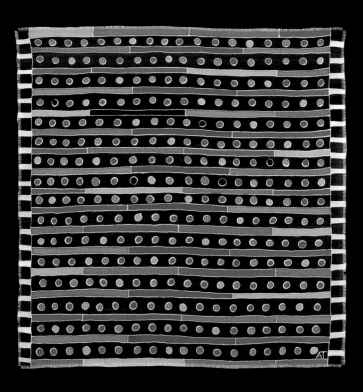

The Fabric Decorator

Foreword by Zandra Rhodes

Sue Peverill

Little, Brown and Company
Boston   Toronto   London

First published in Great Britain in 1988 by Macdonald & Co (Publishers) Ltd

Library of Congress Catalog Card Number
89-84467

Title page: photograph Susanna Price, fabric by Anna Tilson

10 9 8 7 6 5 4 3 2 1

PRINTED IN ITALY

CONTENTS

FOREWORD

When Sue Peverill asked me to write a foreword to *The Fabric Decorator* I was delighted to be involved in a book that had such an inspiring collection of designers' work, and encouraged the braver use of pattern in home textiles, a cause close to my heart.

Textiles are my life. I enjoy the discipline of the prints – the fact that I have to consider measurements and repeats, and that the work combines both technical and artistic elements. In all my textile designs, I am always conscious of the way the printed fabric will be used. I find the fact that the design is directed towards an end product – whether a dress, cushion or sofa – very stimulating. I adore working closely with colours, and throughout my career, right up to my current collection, I have worked, and continue to work, with dyes and printing, making all my own colourways.

My designs are never produced lightly and flippantly, but evolve through an interpretation of my surroundings, seen in my own special way. My first attempts at a design may not work, but they are often essential to the final result. I am never afraid of working with mistakes rather than eliminating them altogether. In fact, during my early years I consciously worked with crude, disquieting colours to produce something new. I maintain my theory that what we find ugly today will be beautiful tomorrow. Likewise, you should never be afraid to experiment – it's the only way to arrive at a design that is truly original and personal. I hope that this book will be the beginning of a journey of excitement and discovery for you, and that you will glean as much enjoyment from textile design as I do.

My Indian feather design
The feather shape lends itself to a border repeat on a textile. I used warm colours and a rich, silky fabric to enhance the exotic tent-like feel of the fabric-covered bed.

6

INTRODUCTION

Evidence of fabric painting has been found as far back as 5,000 BC and it has been an important part of the development of many cultures, widely separated by time and geography. Examples of the technique can be seen on Egyptian murals depicting people wearing clothes decorated with geometric designs in repeat, and hieroglyphics painted on fabric dating from 1514 BC have been found, along with resist-painted fabrics and mordant dyes – a colour-fast natural dye. Records of early fabric printing also exist: block-printing (see Techniques, page 138) is described in historical accounts of the fifth century BC, and is supposed to have emanated from India when the trade routes were opened. It is in India that perhaps the longest continuous history of decorating fabrics with dyes exists. India's success in exporting its printed silks and cottons has had a powerful influence on European fabric design.

Indian circular motif
Religious symbols have been used to decorate the richly coloured and intricately printed Indian fabric shown below. Produced in the eighteenth century, it was hand-printed and hand-dyed.

Indian tree shapes
The type of hand-painted and stencilled cotton shown right was produced in Rajasthan during the seventeenth and eighteenth centuries.

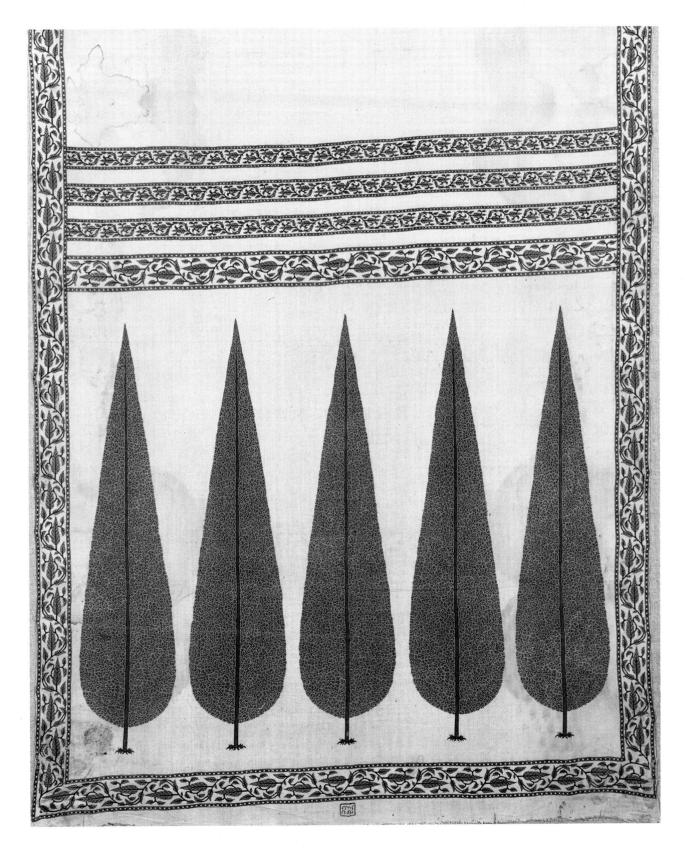

CHINTZES, BATIKS, BLOCK PRINTS AND CALICOES

It was Arab traders, however, who brought the highly prized coloured chintzes to Europe in the second century AD. The name chintz is derived from the Hindu 'chint', which means simply coloured or variegated.

Batik
This Indonesian sarong fabric dates from the early twentieth century.

Almost two centuries later Indian sailors and merchants settled in Java and introduced the wax-resist technique, which later developed into the highly individual batiks we are all familiar with today. These batiks with traditional design motifs are still being produced in Indonesia and successfully exported round the world.

A large number of Indian fabrics dating back to the twelfth century AD are still intact today. Many of these stunningly designed cloths were block-printed with resist and then dyed with either blue (indigo) or red (madder). These two-colour prints were dyed several times and, as a result of the resist, the backgrounds were dyed darker in colour than the motifs, which retained the colour of the original cloth.

By the sixteenth century, Indian fabrics had become more sophisticated and the designs more intricate, increasing further their popularity in Europe. They became known as calicoes, named after the port of Calicut, although we now know calico as a plain woven, cheap cotton. In marked contrast to the earliest resist prints, calicoes were brilliant in colour and the design motifs featured complex patterns of flowers, plants and trees often intertwined with animals or figures. These fabrics were used for wall hangings and bedcovers rather than clothing.

The technique for producing calicoes was as complicated as the designs used to adorn them. A perforated paper stencil was placed over the cloth and charcoal was 'pounced', or pushed, through the holes, leaving a dotted outline once the stencil was removed. Then the outline was painted over with black iron and red dye; indigo was used for blue dye and wax was applied to protect part of the background colour before it was immersed into a dye bath. This process was repeated several times.

Such was the complexity of this process that it took Europeans several decades of experimentation before they could match the technique. It was Indian calicoes that set the standards of design and technical achievement for many years

English fabric detail
A block-printed piece of linen and cotton, designed in England in about 1780.

after their arrival in the West. In fact, it was not until 1770 that the first calico was printed in America.

In 1631, the East India Company was granted permission to import printed cottons into England, and in 1676 William Sherwin received permission to print cottons employing the Indian method of block printing, using engraved wooden blocks. The results were poor imitations of the originals, however, but extremely popular nevertheless.

The success of these fabrics directly threatened the interests of the silk and wool merchants who, in 1700, managed to have the Indian imports banned. Despite the ban, English copies flourished and the use of Indian print designs continued. Opposition from weavers was such that rioting broke out in some traditional cloth-making regions and women were attacked for wearing printed cotton fabrics.

Chinese florals
This hand-painted and printed silk dates from the nineteenth century and was produced for Osterley Park, England.

Despite the opposition, printing continued to develop, and in 1774 permission was granted to print on to pure cotton. In the past, fabrics of inferior quality were usually used for printing.

A significant development at about this time was the development of roller printing, a technique that dramatically increased the output of printed fabric. This marked a transition, for now small-scale designs suitable for clothing were roller printed, while large-scale motifs, suitable for furnishings, continued to be block printed.

New technical innovations continued to increase the choice of patterns, colours and styles available, often at the cost of quality and certainly with a resultant loss of traditional craft skills. This situation was to spur into action, in the second half of the nineteenth century, William Morris, one of the most influential designers of his time (see pages 13-15).

THE CHINESE INFLUENCE ON EUROPE

China's sophisticated early development is evident in its approach to fabric decoration, which was elevated to a significant art form. Although slightly overshadowed by the sophisticated silk weaving and embroidery skills, fabric painting and printing techniques in China were very advanced indeed. Imitators, such as the Japanese, tried to duplicate these designs but, not having the technology to reproduce the exotic animal and bird motifs, they failed to match the Chinese expertise.

With the opening up of trade routes to the East, Chinese fabrics reached Europe, although they were extremely expensive. It was the importation of these fabrics that led to the establishment of an entire industry, which became known as 'Chinoiserie'.

THE ARTS AND CRAFTS MOVEMENT

While William Morris (1834-96), the English painter, printer and designer, embarked on his own design and printing enterprise in 1861, he considered that the standard of design in England, on both the technical and creative levels, was extremely poor. He sought to remedy this situation by becoming one of the most knowledgeable textile historians of his generation. Familiarizing himself with all the modern and ancient printing and painting techniques, Morris started to produce beautifully drawn and painted fabric designs, based on organic forms, flowers and birds, and printed in rich colours. His floral patterns were printed with a new dye known as aniline, which had a brilliance never before available to fabric printers.

Rose and thistle design
This chintz was printed by William Morris in 1882 at the Merton Abbey print works in England.

Largely by his own efforts, Morris elevated the status of textile designer out of the anonymity it had endured in the past. But he was not alone in his interest in and passion for printed fabrics, for Pre-Raphaelite painters such as Ford Madox Brown (1821-93), Rossetti (1828-82) and William Holman Hunt (1827-1910) were also supplying fabric manufacturers with repeating designs. Another making a significant contribution at this time was Owen Jones (1809-74), who produced magnificent designs for the Spitalfields Silk Company owned by Benjamin Warner.

Morris's efforts to produce standards of excellence in both the technical and creative sides of fabric design were very successful. He did not, however, want his designs to become exclusive, and they were manufactured to a high standard for many to buy and enjoy. His designs are still available in stores such as Liberty of London today, just as they were on the day it opened in May, 1875.

The esteem in which British design of this period was held led to the success of ventures such as the Paris Liberty store, where designers worked directly with management, producing commissions for new fabrics which stamped the Liberty image onto the public consciousness. The striking Art Nouveau designs produced under the Liberty banner were the work of designers such as Lindsay Butterfield, Arthur Wilcock and Kay and Arthur Silver of the Silver Studio.

William Morris's work in textiles led to a greater awareness of interior design in general, with more people becoming conscious of their environment and using fabrics more widely in furnishings and furniture. Following on from the Arts and Crafts Movement, in which Morris was a leading figure and pioneer, fabric design became an integral part of every major movement, from the very ornate style of Art Nouveau to the harder-edged designs typical of the Art Deco period.

Fortuny fabric
This hand printed and stencilled fabric was designed by the Italian Mariano Fortuny (1871-1949). Inspired by the Renaissance, Fortuny produced many richly patterned velvets and silks for furnishing and fashion use.

Cray
This block-printed fabric (see p. 138) was designed by William Morris in 1884, and it is still available today. It was named 'Cray' after a tributary of the Thames because of its complex, flowing pattern. Morris took his inspiration from a seventeenth-century design.

THE TWENTIETH CENTURY

The political and social instability of the early twentieth century fuelled the rise of nationalistic identity in design and was the impetus to form organised groups such as the German Deutsche Werkbund (DW). Founded by Herman Mathesius in 1907, the DW's aim was to improve the design of German machine-made products and so break away from English supremacy. These principles were later to be developed by the Bauhaus movement, which produced hand-crafted prototypes destined for mass-production.

The Bauhaus produced a whole range of furniture and fabrics that were simple in their design approach but highly sophisticated, often using subtle colourings and a very original but minimal input in the decoration of fabrics. The Bauhaus was formed by Walter Gropius (1883-1969). As director of the craft and design school he encouraged all forms of design and painting, but particularly architecture. No single textile designer emerges from this movement, since interior designers, furniture designers and painters all designed fabrics, rugs, upholstery and ceramics. Many of these designs are still in production and continue to be a source of inspiration.

In 1903 another group, the Wiener Werkstätte, had been set up by Josef Hoffmann and Koloman Moser. The principle of this organisation was to promote craftsmanship, with designers closely involved throughout the whole manufacturing process. The WW funded workshops where artists could experiment freely, and retained first option to purchase their results.

The WW were a strong influence on mass-produced textiles well into the 1920s, and the introduction of hand-blocked and

Weiner Werkstätte geometrics
Brightly coloured geometric motifs, creating a striped effect, are used in this design, produced by the Weiner Werkstätte workshops, which operated from 1903 to 1932 in Germany.

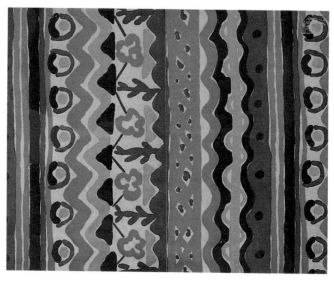

Printed Wiener Werkstätte design
This hand-printed design was carried out at the Weiner Werkstätte workshops (1903-32) in Germany.

painted textiles into their range in 1905 did not in any way alter their existing relationship with manufacturers.

These successes became models for successive organisations such as the Austrian, Swedish and Swiss Werkbund's and the British Design and Industries Association (DIA). This was set up in 1915, and amongst its early members was William Foxton who had for years been advocating, through his textile company, mass-produced artist-designed textiles.

Hoffmann's work with the WW was to be an inspiration for another leading figure of the time – the French designer Paul Poiret. He greatly admired the WW textiles and bought lengths for his 1912 haute couture collection. The inspiration of the WW principles, and his travels in Russia, Germany and middle and eastern Europe, led him to found the Atelier Martine in 1911. He envisaged a school where the pupils, young girls around thirteen years of age, would be encouraged to draw freely and spontaneously from nature. The results were so good that he opened an interior decoration company, Maison Martine, within a few months. The fresh, bold innovations being made under Poiret's auspices were echoed in England's Omega workshops, the brainchild of Roger Fry. These were set up in 1913 to promote the English Post-Impressionist style and to regularly employ artists.

Omega Workshop linen
A mixture of geometric motifs have been hand printed onto this 'Jazz Age' linen fabric, produced at the Omega Workshop in England during the 1920s.

ARTISTS AS DESIGNERS

Many artists have crossed over and designed fabrics, either as one-offs or for commercial production. This tradition is still going on and at the moment seems to be experiencing a revival. Artists are sometimes tempted to fabric design for financial reasons; others see it as a challenge. Many are artists and crafts workers who decorate surfaces for both aesthetic and commercial reasons. Two such artists who have left a fascinating record of their approach to surface decoration are Duncan Grant (1885-1979) and Vanessa Bell (1879-1961).

Grant and Bell moved to Charleston, a large farmhouse in rural Sussex, in 1916. It was a remote and spartan building, but over the course of the following 50 years it was transformed. With their natural talent for mixing patterns with rich colour schemes, Grant and Bell turned Charleston into a wonderful example of how patterns should be used together to create an overall atmosphere. Screens, fabrics, plates, furniture and walls were decorated in their highly individual style. Furniture from the Omega Workshops of Duncan Grant and Roger Fry, some secondhand and some French pieces, all came together when decorated. The halls and passages were the only places left unadorned, providing a contrast to and emphasizing the richness of the rooms leading off.

Although their design work on the house was never commercially reproduced, it has had an influence on craft and design in general and, in particular, on the current decorative revival in crafts such as fabrics and ceramics.

Other artists, such as Sonia Delauney (1885-1979) and Raoul Dufy (1877-1953), designed fabrics for the worlds of fashion and furnishings. In the style of their paintings, they produced fabric for exclusive fashion houses in limited quantities as well as designs for the mass market. Sonia Delauney printed scarves and plates, and designed backdrops and costumes for the theatre, using her design skills to encompass every area for a totally co-ordinated look. Dufy collaborated with the fashion designer Paul Poiret on dress and furnishing fabrics, many of which were hand-painted or hand-blocked.

The idea of artists as fabric designers, bringing their unique visual images and original uses of colour to the area of textiles, was not overlooked by Zika Ascher (1909-), a textile printer and designer who commissioned many artists to design for him. Always one to encourage young talent, one of his most adventurous projects was in the 1940s when he comissioned designs from a series of famous artists. This collaboration resulted in magnificent hand-printed panels by Henri Matisse (1869-1954)

Duncan Grant design
This fabric was hand printed by Duncan Grant for the Omega Workshop, London, England.

18

Sailing boats
This abstract design was specially commissioned by Zika Ascher from Antoni Clare in 1947. It was hand-screen printed on to rayon.

and Henry Moore (1898-1986), plus a range of scarves by such distinguished artists as Barbara Hepworth (1903-75), Graham Sutherland (1903-80), and Alexander Calder (1898-1973). These designs were somewhat ahead of their time, but Zika Ascher was, and still is, happy to experiment and find new ways to make fabric printing more exciting.

In the 1950s the Ascher company provided fabric for designers such as Givenchy, St Laurent and Dior. Many of these fabrics were new and experimental, from large-scale florals to abstract designs on paper dresses for Ossie Clark in the mid-1960s. Designers such as Zika Ascher, Zandra Rhodes (see page 47) and Celia Birtwell (see page 68), and shops such as Liberty and Heal's, have all helped to encourage a wider interest in fabric design, whether for fashion or furnishings.

Over the last few years this interest has led to many textile designers setting up small workshops and painting and printing highly individual pieces of work. Some textile artists produce 'one-off' wall hangings (see page 108-15), while others work in a more commercial way, selling limited amounts of hand-printed fabric to fashion designers or small shops.

In the area of textiles there is a fine line between artist, designer and craftsperson. Some produce fabrics for other designers to use, while others rely on exhibitions and galleries to sell their work. A recent trend has been for designers to work directly with interior designers, co-ordinating hand-painted fabrics with furniture in room settings. Sometimes designers work in a variety of areas, crossing over into the commercial market – perhaps producing highly individual pieces of work by applying the paint directly on the fabric and then interpreting these designs on to paper, building up a collection of more commercial work for sale to fabric manufacturers.

This book shows the work of a selection of those highly individual and original artists and designers, operating in an area that is so often unfairly neglected and one that certainly deserves the attention of a wider audience.

White rose design
Many well-known artists have, in the past, designed textiles for the mass market. This design was produced by Graham Sutherland in 1940.

BASICS

There is virtually no limit to the variety of designs that can be created by hand painting or printing fabric. And any type of cloth can be decorated in this way, since commercial fabric paints are suitable for both natural and man-made materials.

Over the last few years the trend in furnishings has moved towards natural fibres, although these have always been favoured by fabric designers since they take the paint and dye so well. Another reason for choosing natural fibres is that since you have taken the time and effort to paint a unique pattern on to a piece of fabric, then the fabric itself should look and feel as good as the design. Natural fibres, such as silk, cotton, wool and linen, and man-made fibres, such as terylene, polyester and nylon, are listed in the fabric guide (see page 152).

No matter how easy the fabric painting or printing technique, it is essential that you use the correct combination of 'ingredients' in order to achieve a successful result. This chapter outlines the fabrics, paints and basic procedures you need to be familiar with before you start.

BEFORE YOU PAINT

Circus design
Yvonne Chambers used a simple brush-stroke technique to paint this satin fabric. When using a brush-stroke technique it is best to be spontaneous – don't be tentative or hesitate too much. A nervous, hesitant hand will produce an unprofessional wobbly line. Also, do not overload the paintbrush with too much fabric paint, since the motifs will look better if they are slightly drier and look more like what they are – brush strokes – rather than thick, heavy stripes. Texture and highlights were added with fabric crayon. The design was used to cover a dressing table (see page 82).

Before starting to paint any surface, the following guidelines must be considered. Firstly, you should work out a suitable design for your scheme and select the colours to be used. Secondly, make sure that you choose a fabric that will enhance the design. Thirdly, take care to use the most suitable fabric paint, taking into account both the nature of the design and your preferred fabric. And finally, find the easiest method to achieve the desired effect.

As an example, a soft floral design in pastel shades would call for a smooth silk or a fine cotton, and a suitable method of decoration might be stencilling, perhaps using a pearlized fabric paint. If, on the other hand, the design is to be a random, textured pattern in vibrant colours, then perhaps an inexpensive calico or canvas would be more appropriate. An opaque fabric paint and a combination of three simple techniques, such as spattering, sponging and painting bold geometric shapes freehand with a household paintbrush, could be used to create this type of design.

DRAWING AND PLANNING THE DESIGN

If the design is a textured, all-over one with no regular shapes, then your main concern will be the colours. The easiest painting techniques for this are sponging and spattering. Both of these methods can be tried out on paper first, or on scraps of fabric, in different colour combinations.

Bear in mind that you are creating all-over random textures, not regular patterns. Regular patterns need to be planned, these don't. Keep a note of colour combinations, how many are used and how they were mixed, since it is difficult to chance upon the same colours again if you have no reference for colour matching. Colours will overlap each other, creating new ones each time, so make sure you find these acceptable.

If you have chosen a more formal design idea, make rough sketches on paper until you are completely satisfied. Start by using a pencil and then fill in areas of colour with crayons or felt-tip pens. For a more accurate colour version, mix up shades that you might actually apply, using powder paints, poster colour or a gouache. At this stage it does not have to be too accurate or perfectly painted, since it is intended just to give you an indication of how the finished design might look.

The next stage is to draw the design to scale. To square up a design, draw a square grid either on an existing design sketch or on a piece of tracing paper that is large enough to fit over the sketch. To make it larger or smaller, either copy the drawing on to dressmakers' pattern paper or draw it on to your own grid.

Carefully transfer the design from the original onto your grid one square at a time, making sure that all lines and motifs that make up the design appear in exactly the same place in a large square as they did in a small one.

Photocopying design ideas can be useful to repeat motifs in different pattern arrangements. Many photocopiers are capable of enlarging images as well. This will enable you to check that the motifs work well together and that the proportions of the design are correct. You will also be able to see if the colours are evenly distributed or if one colour is dominating the rest. Graph paper can be used if the design is a border or if it repeats in a very regular way.

If you lack drawing skills, motifs can be traced from virtually anywhere – don't overlook sources like a wall or a piece of china as well as the more usual ones such as fabrics, books or magazines. When tracing, make sure the tracing paper completely covers the design area. Use a hard pencil, since this will give a sharper line and will not smudge so readily.

Abstract colour
Annie Sherburne used specially dyed felt for this brightly coloured abstract.

COTTON FABRICS

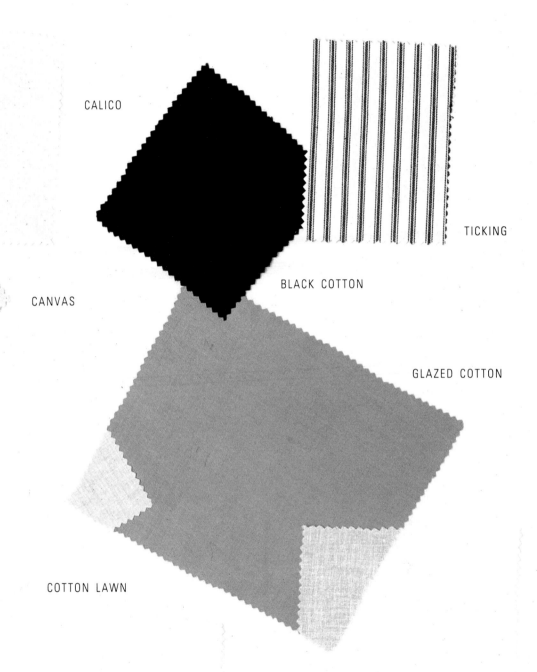

CALICO

TICKING

CANVAS

BLACK COTTON

GLAZED COTTON

COTTON LAWN

COTTON VOILE

WHITE COTTON

OTHER FABRICS

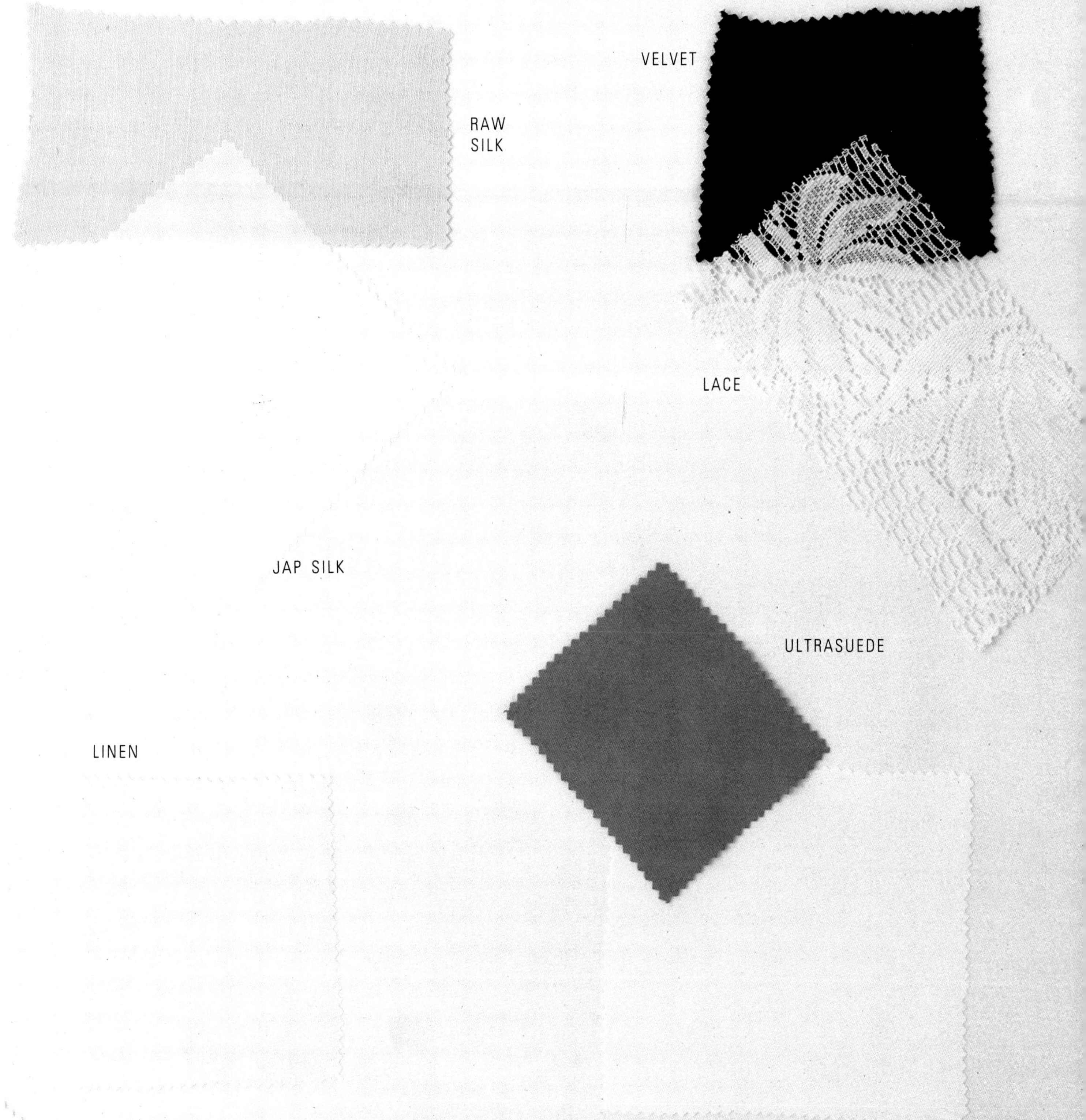

RAW SILK

VELVET

LACE

JAP SILK

ULTRASUEDE

LINEN

POLYESTER

For details of the fabrics shown, see the Fabric Guide, pages 152-3.

FABRIC PAINTS

Use standard fabric paints from the jar, mixed to create new colours, diluted for colourwash effects or mixed with white to make pastels. Special silk paints can only be used on silk fabrics. See the Paint Guide, pages 152-5.

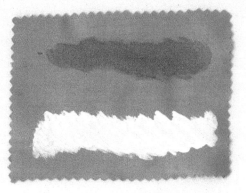

STANDARD PAINT ON GLAZED COTTON

STANDARD PAINT ON WHITE COTTON

STANDARD PAINT ON CANVAS

STANDARD PAINT ON BLACK COTTON

STANDARD PAINT ON CALICO

STANDARD PAINT ON COTTON VOILE

STANDARD PAINT ON TICKING

SILK
PAINT ON
RAW SILK

SILK PAINT ON RAW SILK

SILK PAINT ON
JAP SILK

STANDARD PAINT ON RAW SILK

STANDARD PAINT ON JAP SILK

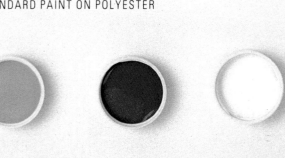

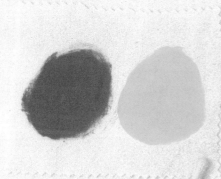

STANDARD PAINT ON POLYESTER

STANDARD PAINT ON
LINEN

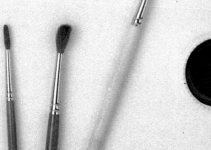

FABRIC PENS

Felt-tipped fabric pens give fine and thick lines, and are particularly useful when drawing outlines. Although suitable for any fabric, felt pens won't show up on dark-coloured materials. See the Paint Guide, pages 152-5.

COTTON LAWN

WHITE COTTON

CANVAS

COTTON VOILE

GLAZED COTTON

CALICO

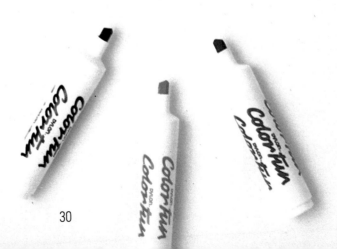

LINEN

TICKING

POLYESTER

RAW SILK

JAP SILK

FABRIC CRAYONS

Drawn directly onto any fabric, the effect of fabric crayons is the same as that of conventional crayons. The texture will vary with the fabric. See also the Paint Guide, pages 152-5.

FABRIC CRAYON ON
GLAZED COTTON

FABRIC CRAYON ON COTTON

FABRIC CRAYON ON BLACK COTTON

FABRIC CRAYON ON CALICO

FABRIC CRAYON ON VOILE

FABRIC CRAYON ON CANVAS

FABRIC CRAYON ON COTTON LAWN

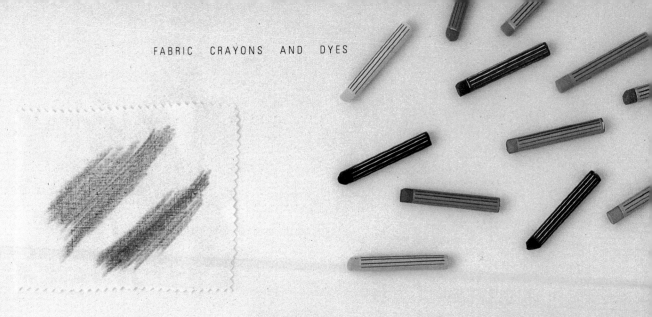

DYES

Over-dyeing already printed or woven fabrics can give a new lease of life to a dull, faded fabric. Natural fabrics take dye very well, but most synthetics are unsuitable. See also dyeing, page 150.

FABRIC CRAYON ON JAP SILK

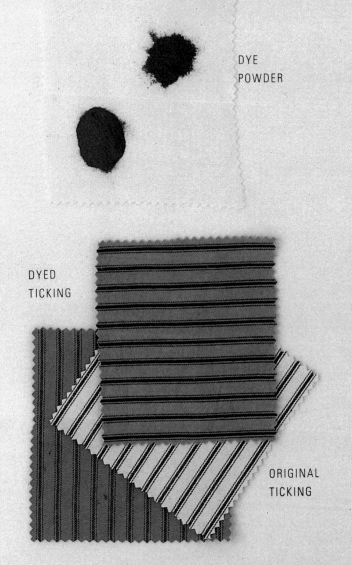

DYE POWDER

FABRIC CRAYON ON RAW SILK

DYED TICKING

ORIGINAL TICKING

FABRIC CRAYON ON VELVET

33

EQUIPMENT AND WORKSPACE

It is best to start with leftover fabric or old sheets. Also, department stores often sell off remnants of good quality fabric extremely cheaply. For a beginner, buying an expensive fabric to paint can be daunting, since too much time can be spent fretting about making a mistake and thus ruining the material. Move on to more expensive fabrics only when you have mastered a few of the basic techniques and feel more confident in your ability. Starting with the easy techniques is not necessarily a handicap – often the simplest of designs and techniques can be the most stunning.

BUYING AND USING FABRIC PAINTS

As a guide to buying the right quantity of paint, one small pot will give all-over coverage to the average-size cushion cover. This advice does depend, though, on the technique used, since some require more paint than others. With stencilling, for example, the brush should be used quite dry and the paint only dabbed on, making it very economical. Spattering, however, uses quite a lot as the effect is one of splashing on paint.

A golden rule is that you should make sure you mix sufficient paint of each colour to finish your design. Even experienced professionals find it difficult to match exactly a mixed colour, and even a slight variation may spoil the overall effect. If too much paint is mixed, store it in an airtight jar as fabric paint has quite a long life.

All liquid fabric colours are intermixable, so an infinite number of hues is possible. To save on the expense of buying too many basic colours, a palette of red, blue, yellow, orange, black and white would be a good starting point for any new fabric painter. You will find that white is particularly useful for creating pastel colours. Bear in mind that you should always add colour to white, not the other way round, in order to achieve successful pale shades.

BASIC EQUIPMENT AND PROCEDURES

Once you have decided upon the design and the colours you are going to use, make sure the correct equipment is at hand.

■ Always have clean water available, and change it frequently. It is important to keep colours 'clean', therefore washing brushes between colour changes is vital. Squeeze excess water from the brushes: if the brush is too wet when dipped in the paint it will bleed colour on to the fabric – disastrous if straight lines and hard edges are required.

■ You should have lots of paper for blotting excess paint and for covering any vulnerable surfaces, such as carpets.

Sponging
This technique can be carried out in one or more colours (see page 127), and the only tool required is a natural marine sponge.

Spattering
One of the simplest techniques to execute (see page 130) – a flick of the wrist gives fabric a Jackson Pollock look.

34

■ You will need a selection of brushes for different techniques – from fine ones for intricate areas to household types for bold brushstrokes. You may also need to buy specialist types such as stencil brushes.

■ Make sure you have a large enough flat surface to work on and cover it with an old blanket before starting. This will act as a backing cloth and absorb any excess paint.

■ Always remove any manufacturer's finish or dressing if the fabric is new. Do this by washing or dry cleaning the fabric, otherwise the paints will not take very well. Make sure the fabric is clean, dry and crease free. If necessary, use masking tape to stretch the edges fairly taut. Also, have clean rag at hand for mopping up any blobs.

■ Have all the paints ready mixed in appropriately sized saucers or jars.

■ For precise outlining you may prefer to buy fabric felt-tip pens (see page 30). These are easier to control than a brush, and they can be used with a ruler for additional accuracy. Test the pens on different types of fabric since they may bleed or spread on silky surfaces.

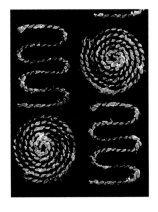

Block printing
Everyday household materials such as string can be used for this dramatic but easy technique (see page 138).

■ It might sound obvious, but make sure you have enough space to finish a design, and that the light is good. Colours can look totally different in natural light as opposed to electric light.

■ Open windows if possible – all fabric paints are non-toxic, but the movement of air will speed up the drying process.

■ Have a hairdryer to hand – for very wet areas of paint, you will have to blot up any excess and then use a hairdryer held 15-30 cm (6-12 in) away from the surface. (Always leave the fabric in the same position, preferably flat, until it is completely dry. That way you do not run the risk of smudging the design.)

■ Once the colours are mixed and all the other equipment is ready, check that the fabric is secure. If the back and front are to be painted, place paper on polythene between the layers of fabric to prevent the paint seeping through to the other side.

■ Most fabric paints require heat to make them permanent once they have been painted, so always leave them to dry after painting and cover the ironing board with a clean piece of fabric or paper before fixing the design. Set the iron to medium-hot and press the fabric for a few minutes according to the paint manufacturers' instructions.

Spraying
This subtle diffused effect needs a little practice (see page 128), but once mastered it is quick to do.

Stencilling
A simple way to decorate fabric with motifs is to use a stencil (see page 132).

THE PAINTING SEQUENCE

No matter what technique you decide to use, it is important to tackle the job in a logical sequence. You should start by painting the lightest colour first and work through to the darker shades. And try to work from top to bottom to avoid smudging the still wet paint. If more than one colour is used on the same motif, let the first one dry before painting with the next colour. This will avoid any possibility of the colours merging into each other. If the first coat of fabric paint is patchy, leave it to dry before applying another coat. Again, do not overload the brush with paint; it is better to use too little than too much and risk unnecessary blobs.

Once the design is finished, you can always add extra texture or motifs, such as dots or textured rubbings, using felt-tip pens or fabric crayons (see pages 30-2).

Mistakes do happen, but this does not necessarily mean disaster, since they can sometimes be incorporated into a design by adding another motif. As these fabrics are unique, mistakes can often just be left – the occasional eccentric 'splash' of colour will not spoil the overall design.

Whatever the design, it is vital to follow any manufacturer's instructions concerning fabric paints and fixing.

BASIC PAINTING METHODS

If you want to become a good fabric artist, you should continually experiment, playing with different shapes, equipment and colour, and develop imaginative new techniques and methods as you progress. Leave the harder, more technical designs and techniques until you have had quite a lot of practice.

Sometimes, specialist equipment is necessary, but mostly you can make do with ordinary household items – especially with these basic painting methods. As an example, when painting a design that has straight edges, such as a geometric pattern, stick masking tape round the edge of the shape and paint inside the tape. Leave the paint to dry before removing the tape.
Spattering This is by far the easiest technique – all that is necessary in the way of equipment is a brush or stick loaded with fabric paint: a flick of the wrist sends the paint, hopefully, in the right direction. Because this can be messy, space is an important consideration. It is not a good idea, for example, to spatter a duvet cover if you live in a bed-sit. With this technique it is possible to make a mistake, so wear old clothing and cover the surrounding area with masses of protective paper. If possible, it is a good idea to work outside. Instructions on the method are given on page 130.

Transfer printing
With this technique you draw the design on paper, then iron it onto the fabric (see page 140). This allows you to cut out or scrap mistakes, and so avoid wasting fabric.

Simple paint effects
The cushions and the table surface have been co-ordinated using a spattering technique (see page 130).

Sponging Paint sponged over fabric for a textured effect is simple too. The best results are achieved by using a natural sea sponge. Since these are expensive you could substitute a synthetic household sponge or a screwed-up piece of muslin. Instructions on the method are given on page 127.

Spraying Although this effect looks very professional, and therefore difficult, in fact it is quite easy. An old toothbrush or garden spray is useful for a sprayed effect, although a spray diffuser can be bought very cheaply. Specialist equipment for spraying, such as airbrushes or spray guns, can be expensive. Instructions on the method are given on page 128.

Block printing Objects such as forks, matchboxes and rope stuck to card or wood can be used to create interesting shapes. Although this approach might seem a little too basic, if it is used in the appropriate design and with the right combination of colours, the results can look extremely effective. Instructions on the method are given on page 138.

Stencilling This is a simple way of producing motifs if you lack drawing skills. Start with a bought stencil and use a single colour until you master the technique. Instructions on the method are given on page 132.

PATTERN

STYLE

AND COLOUR

The aspects of fabric decoration to do with pattern, style and colour are, in some ways, the most difficult to provide guidance on, since they are so concerned with personal tastes and preferences. Also, what needs to be borne in mind is the setting in which the fabric will be used, and the use to which it will be put. The types of pattern and colour combinations appropriate for a child's room, for example, will be worlds apart from the style you will be trying to achieve in your own bedroom or sitting room. In much the same way, the type of fabric you choose to work on will impart its own characteristics to the colours and patterns applied: the soft, flowing folds of fine cottons and silks demand a different treatment to the stiffer, coarser and more textured surfaces of calicoes and canvas.

The most important lesson to be learnt from this chapter is the need for patience and experimentation. You have, after all, a whole history of design motifs and patterns at your disposal, readily available in magazines, illustrated books, art galleries and the like. Inspiration is all around you, all you need is the interest and the imagination.

INSPIRATION
FOR FABRIC DESIGNS

When it comes to decorating, the use of fabric is undoubtedly an easy way to transform a room, especially when the design of the fabric is unique. Fabric can be used to change the shape of a window or the look of a piece of furniture, and it can be a cheap and easy way of revamping a tired looking interior. Painting an original design on to a piece of fabric can in itself create a distinct atmosphere, giving an ordinary, even uninspiring, room a refreshingly individual designer look.

Clothes are changed frequently for special occasions, to suit our daily requirements or just because fashion dictates that a particular style is no longer acceptable. But using colour and pattern in the home is more difficult, and we will agonize over fabrics, furniture and colour choice for some considerable time, hoping to make the right decision. Although fashion does influence home decoration, the change is not so radical or so frequent as in fashion clothes. The time and cost incurred in choosing colours and patterns to live with would deter the most enthusiastic decorator from changing colour schemes too often.

Choosing the right combination of colours and patterns depends on your final goal – whether you want to create a total

Colour and shape
Malcolm Temple hand painted bold, primary-coloured and geometric shapes onto canvas to produce this dramatic screen.

Screen printed vase motif
Sally Guy used only two colours for this simple hand-printed motif. However, screen printing (see page 144) is the most complicated technique, so don't tackle it before trying some of the simpler methods.

look or to breathe new life into your existing decor by 'accessorizing'. If you feel less than confident about attempting some of the more complex ideas illustrated in this book, it is always best to start off with a simple one and then build on it as your confidence increases.

The best way to find out whether colours, effects and patterns work together is to try them out. Restrictions of cost may limit the amount of money and effort put into experimenting, but this need not be a handicap. For a beginner, certain limitations can be a relief, since colour and design are made easier when choice is limited.

If you are somebody who has definite ideas on what you want, and therefore have no problems when it comes to deciding how a room or a piece of fabric should look, this book should be used as a source of inspiration and to expand on the ideas you already have. For those who are less sure of what they want, this book can assist in the choosing of colours and patterns, and offer advice on how to use them in the context of a furnishing scheme.

Subtle colours
Colours don't have to be clear primaries to be strong. Here, Jasia Szerszynska has mixed soft but strong blues, greens and yellows to create a subtle combination.

COLOUR AND PATTERN

Colour contrast
Bright colours on a black background produce a vibrant result that is particularly suited to silk. Frannie used a resist method to paint the flowers (see page 136).

Colour, since it can make or break a design, seems to be the most difficult area to decide on. Colours provide an atmosphere: they can be warm or cool, pale or dark, expansive or enclosing. There are no longer any rules governing how colour should be used. No colour is ever looked at in isolation; colours are always perceived with others, and so you should take into account the effect of different combinations.

Strong colours such as bright greens, reds and black can have an exhilarating effect when used with other colours, but used in large blocks they can be overpowering. However, black and white, used as a total look, can create a powerful and exciting atmosphere (see pages 52-3).

To a certain extent, our surroundings dictate which colours are acceptable. If the room is small, with limited natural light, then pastel shades will tend to give the room depth and warmth. On the other hand, a large, bright room could be painted stark white, with colour added from fabrics or other accessories. Think carefully when painting fabric to tone in with the existing decor – large-scale geometric designs in primary colours, for example, may look out of place in a pastel-coloured room dominated by floral motifs.

Colourful geometrics
Anna Tilson combined bright colours with black and white for this simple but striking pattern.

Try taking your favourite colours as a starting point, and then gradually add small amounts of other colours to see if they work well together. Another approach is to use shades and tones of one particular favourite colour; this can be as interesting as any multicoloured combination.

Neutral colours are often the easiest to add to. A cream or white room will look just as effective if pastel colours, primaries or just one other colour is used. Each colour combination will produce a different effect on the room and create unique atmosphere. Ultimately, this is where decisions have to be made concerning which one is the most acceptable to live with. It is often

Classical colours
Gold on royal blue gives a regal mood to this screen printed classical repeat by Annie Doherty.

Colour and texture
Annie Sherburne used specially dyed felt as a base for this abstract pattern.

difficult to say why a colour works best with one shade and not with another.

There have been plenty of books written on the subject of colour theory and psychology, and many artists have spent their lives exploring the effects that different colours have on one another. It may be an idea to take a brief look at some books on colour theory, but don't get too involved in the theoretical side. It is just as beneficial to visit galleries and exhibitions, or just browse through the many art books available and find inspiration in the colours used by celebrated artists. For example, Mondrian's use of blocks of colour with black or grey line could easily be adapted to a painted textile. And the colours and brushstrokes of Van Gogh's work could inspire a bold floral motif.

Combining colours
This striking hand-printed
fabric by Sally Guy combines
colour and black and white
effectively.

IDEAS AND INSPIRATION

On a more down-to-earth level, look at the world around you. Why does the flower stall seem so appealing with its riot of colours and patterns? Nature manages to achieve perfect colour combinations; from the rich and varied tones of autumn leaves to the clear pastels of sweet peas. Take notice of colour schemes in stores and restaurants, and make a note of any that particularly catch your eye as well as those that have not been successful. Think about why those schemes failed. Wander round department stores looking at colours and fabrics.

Collect any scraps of fabric that you are particularly attracted to, keeping plain as well as patterned types and different qualities – sheer and opaque, for example – and play around with different colour combinations. Experiment by choosing one colour and adding a very small amount of another, then change to putting equal amounts of each colour together to see the difference. It is also a good idea to try out the various fabric paints on these scraps so that you experiment with different textures and coloured backgrounds.

For another excellent source of inspiration, look at magazines devoted to interior design. Keep cuttings of any designs, patterns and colour schemes that you could possibly use or adapt. If something particularly appeals, why not copy it? Live with your ideas for a while; pin them to the wall or to a piece of furniture. Make sure they look as good at night as they do during the day. Now is the time to find out whether you can actually live with that particular design or colour.

INTERPRETING YOUR IDEAS

Once your colour choices have been made, drawing skills may come into play. When looking through this book the comment 'I couldn't possibly do that' could be repeated all too often. To be realistic, in some cases this is true. A few of the designs shown are purely inspirational, produced to show just what can be achieved in the area of decoration. Most of the designers whose work is shown in this book have had years of training and practice, and trying to emulate their technical skills would be difficult for a beginner. But take heart, not all techniques are difficult: painted effects, for example, require no drawing skills whatsoever. Most people are now familiar with the popular painted effects for walls and woodwork, and have seen how they can be used to transform a room. Many of these techniques translate just as successfully on to fabric. For example, a lightly sponged loose cover in pastel shades with contrasting spattered cushions will look stunning and give individuality to any setting.

Muted colours with black
Soft blue, grey and light
yellow, though muted
colours, have impact when
combined with black, as in
this hand-printed fabric by
Annie Doherty.

Of course, you can use the same techniques to achieve different looks by changing the background colour or the fabric. A sponged piece of silk is going to look very different to a sponged piece of canvas. You should consider these points before you start, so that you don't waste time and money.

Although sponging (see page 127) and spattering (see page 130) are very simple and attractive enough in their own right, they can also be used to provide interesting backgrounds on which to overlay a stencilled motif (see page 132). Stencilled motifs can be traced, copied or even bought ready cut, and they will help those without technical design skills to achieve a professional finish quite easily. Most stencil motifs can be used in a linear manner to create a border or applied at intervals as an overall design.

Tracing motifs from a piece of fabric can be a method of decorating a lampshade, cushion or blind so that it co-ordinates with that fabric. To use a multicoloured, multipatterned fabric twice in the same room might look overpowering. But a small motif taken from the fabric and then repeated allows fabric and accessories to work well together.

Painter's colours
Laura Stirling used a rich
mixture of colours to create
this painterly effect.

45

LEARNING FROM DESIGNERS

Classical imagery
Black and white is very effective with classical imagery, as Timney-Fowler have found. This detailed screen-printed square was produced using a photographic technique.

Established designers such as Timney-Fowler and Zandra Rhodes draw their inspiration in much the same way as suggested on page 44. They still have the same design problems to solve, albeit on a much grander scale.

The designs of Timney-Fowler are easily recognizable by their bold use of black and white. Limiting the use of colour can be cost effective, as well as allowing more freedom in the choice of designs. Other colours don't 'get in the way' of Timney- Fowler's extraordinary imagery, which is often inspired by classical Greek motifs and architectural features. Their designs manage to look contemporary and traditional, depending on how they are used.

It would be difficult, if not impossible, to hand paint fabric to achieve a similar effect. Although the fabrics of both designers are screen-printed by hand in limited quantities, a lot of technical equipment goes into producing them (see page 144). However, they can still be learnt from. The use of strong imagery in one colour can provide a definite theme for a whole room or just a cushion or an upholstered piece of furniture.

The fabrics of Zandra Rhodes are recognized throughout the world by their rich use of colour and original design motifs. She has always found inspiration for her fabrics all around her. A jewel-coloured fabric with a beautifully intricate design may have started out as a drawing of a few rocks or pebbles. Such is her imagination, she can see the design potential in almost anything. Most of us cannot match her talent, but we can learn

Timney-Fowler
These designers have a very distinctive style, inspired by classical imagery. They produce hand-printed fabrics and co-ordinated home furnishings.

Zandra Rhodes' fabrics
Contrasting designs linked by colour and Zandra Rhodes' personal style work well together. These furnishing fabrics are hand screen printed.

from the way in which she produces her designs.

Zandra Rhodes has always travelled, and this has been a constant source of ideas for her many fabric collections. She takes inspiration from traditional imagery as well as from the landscape of countries such as Mexico, Australia, America, Greece and India. She makes many preliminary sketches and doodles and collects information and memorabilia that may be incorporated into one of her designs.

Only by experimenting – tearing up the designs and rearranging them, or reducing and enlarging the size with a change of colour, background or an extra motif added here or there, for example – will a satisfactory design solution be reached. Many sketches, paintings and colourways later, the finished fabric will be produced.

Starting with a favourite colour or fabric for inspiration is an easy way to develop an idea, using patterns to minimize or maximize effect, and thus create your own individual style. Style is not something that can be bought, but it can be acquired with help – although, of course, you may have natural instinct for it. Style is a means of self-expression, but even those who have plenty of ideas may not always know how to achieve an end result. To be successful, you must plan your design carefully and decide what effect you want and how best to achieve it. And you must master the technical side – many a good idea has been spoilt by sloppy application.

LEARNING FROM NATURE

Combining images
Unusual, or even odd, combinations of motifs are worth trying – on this fabric Sara Robbins has hand printed a border of flowers and hands.

Florals are always a popular theme, either in the form of a 'country garden' style featuring a mixture of different types of floral patterns in one room, or in the form of a simple, stencilled floral motif repeated as an all-over pattern or used as a border.

Still on the floral theme, another idea is to use silk paints to create a slightly abstract, but pretty flower design utilizing a watercolour technique. This will allow the soft, flowing colours to merge harmoniously into each other. This is a good example of a situation where the fabric and the paints must be compatible. A fine, smooth silk is a perfect background for watery silk paints, whereas the effect would be totally lost on canvas.

Utilizing nature's assets has always been a universal source of inspiration, and each season conjures up different elements

Traditional motifs
This screen-printed fabric by Gabrielle Bolton uses traditional design in a contemporary way: the bunches of flowers parody the traditional paisley motif. A simple leaf print in a reverse colourway would co-ordinate well with this fabric.

that can be exploited. Photographs or sketches can be used of scenes or details to generate ideas for painted borders or stencilled cushions. A single vase of tulips, for example, is a good choice: the simple flower shapes and straight stems in a variety of bright colours easily lend themselves to stylized interpretation. As the seasons change, autumn leaves are an inspiration in themselves, particularly for the range and variety of colours they offer. Shells are another good source of design ideas. The combination of delicate colours and definite, decorative shapes makes them an ideal subject for fabric painting. Ideally, you should collect or buy real shells, rather than working from a photograph. The fabric paints must be mixed as near to the natural colouring of the shells as possible – the whole effect could be ruined by using harsh, inappropriate colours. For a truly exquisite effect, try painting the shells on a fine cotton or silk. A good place to use fabric painting is in a children's room (see pages 116-123), since themes are often quite obvious. Animals

Fish and flower
Sara Robbins has combined floral and animal motifs very successfully in this hand-printed fabric by using geometric borders to define the different motifs.

Combining nature with geometrics
Frannie combined a simple fish motif with geometric shapes on this hand-painted silk (see page 136).

are always a good choice, as they play such an important part in most children's lives. Try painting animal prints as they are easier to portray than the animal shapes themselves. Look closely at leopard and dalmation spots or tiger and zebra stripes, and then focus in on one shape. The shape is actually quite simple, just a blob or a stripe. Repeat it in various sizes over an area to create the right impression.

GEOMETRIC AND ABSTRACT PATTERNS

Abstract repeat
Sally Guy used a simple shape in different sizes to create a more complex-looking pattern. The wide border adds to the impact of this strong design.

Geometric themes are often very striking. Apart from bold stripes and checks, look at the work of some modern artists such as Kandinsky, Miro and Picasso, to see how they use shape and colour. You might be inspired to create your own artist-influenced fabric on either a blind or, on a smaller scale, on cushions and lampshades.

Geometric and abstract patterns were first brought into common use in the 1930s. Influenced by the abstract painters of the time, geometrics became popular rendered in subtle colours to suit the decor of existing interiors and tone down the severity of the otherwise overpowering hard edges. The thirties period of design is known as Art Deco, and it is a wonderful source of geometric design inspiration.

Geometric designs don't, however, always have to be on a large scale. They can be equally effective used as a border, or on blinds, cushions and bed linen. Geometrics can also be softened by the addition of curves or the introduction of a floral motif. Some geometrics can create a stark atmosphere. But for a less dramatic effect, try using a simple chequerboard pattern or a broad shape in a single colour. A more complicated design, using many motifs in strong colours, would be best suited to a blind, where the surface remains flat and therefore the design is not distorted.

Cushions also represent an ideal surface for geometric designs. A small area to work on is far more manageable and the design permutations are endless. Cushion designs can be as elaborate as you like, since a group of cushions does not necessarily have to co-ordinate with the rest of the decor – it can,

Lines and dashes
Simple geometrics, like this pattern by Paul Wearing, can be extremely effective if executed in strong colour combinations. To create this effect paint white lines freehand onto black cloth.

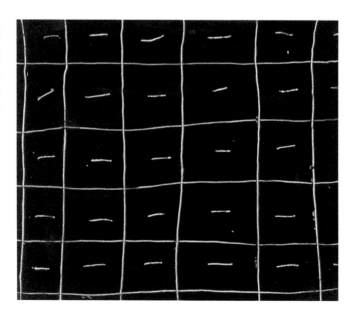

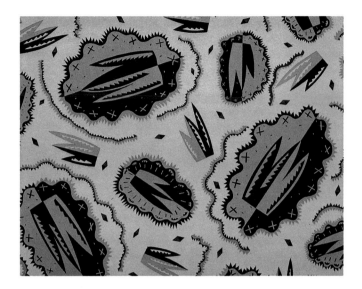

instead, be a unique addition to a fairly plain setting.

As with all fabric painting, you must ensure that the design and the fabric are compatible. A heavily textured surface will spoil the hard edges a geometric requires to be effective – the results will be fuzzy instead of crisp and clean. Choose a firm, closely woven material for this type of design.

Using spray paints (the type used for retouching autos, see page 155) is an easy way to achieve a good finish. But here again your choice of fabric is important, since this type of paint is really suitable only for fabrics that are seldom or never washed. A heavy canvas fabric that is intended for a deckchair, or stiff Holland that will be made up into a blind are both ideal for this treatment.

If the appropriate paints are used, geometric designs can work well when painted on to silk. The resist method (see pages 136-7) will soften the edges slightly and prevent the design looking too severe, while still providing that important visual impact.

Strong geometric designs in primary colours will have real punch on a large area of fabric, such as that found on a sofa, especially if the room is fairly neutral with lots of space and light. For a sofa, it is important that you paint the fabric before it is made up. Also, it is vital that you position the fabric so that the pattern matches all the way across and in the different sections of the sofa.

Geometric shapes are not always inspired by modern art or contemporary design ideas. A simple motif, such as a classical Greek key, can easily be used on a border. For this, simple basic techniques such as block printing or stencilling can be used (see pages 138 and 132).

Abstract pattern
Paul Wearing used graphic imagery in a strong but unusual colourway for this hand-printed fabric.

USING BLACK AND WHITE

The most striking colour combinations are often the most obvious – and there cannot be a more dominant colour contrast than black and white. Whatever the style of the pattern, if painted or printed in black and white it will immediately become the focus of attention in a room setting.

Geometrics (see page 50) in black and white were extremely popular in the 1960s, for both clothes design and furnishings. Artists such as Bridget Riley and Vaserely greatly popularized this style of imagery, which became known as Op Art. But che-querboard patterns have been used throughout history in one form or another. This simple but effective use of squares always makes a strong statement, whether used as a border or as tiles covering a large area.

Using black on white or white on black has advantages beyond the economical use of fabric paint; the limited colour can make design decisions easier. A complicated design with many components is far easier to work out with such a limited palette at your disposal. Black and white themes are ideal for canvas; if used on a fine silk, however, black could look very messy. A household paintbrush dipped in black fabric paint and applied to cotton or canvas in a stripe or simple check can look striking (see page 76).

Repeating motif
Lucy Clive used graphic black and white to emphasise this dramatic hand-printed motif.

Using a large motif
Joanna Beale has printed this fabric with a large-scale motif that makes a strong impression when executed in black and white.

Outline image
This powerful image, hand printed by Lucy Clive, is influenced by centuries of patterning.

Teacup pattern
Sally Guy used bold simple shapes with combinations of black and white to create a bright modern look. As an alternative colourway, try black with a strong primary colour such as yellow.

PERIOD STYLES

Traditional style
Miroslava used rich colours
and traditional colours on a
dark ground for this
sumptuous hand block-
printed (see page 138) fabric.
The motifs have an antique
glass quality.

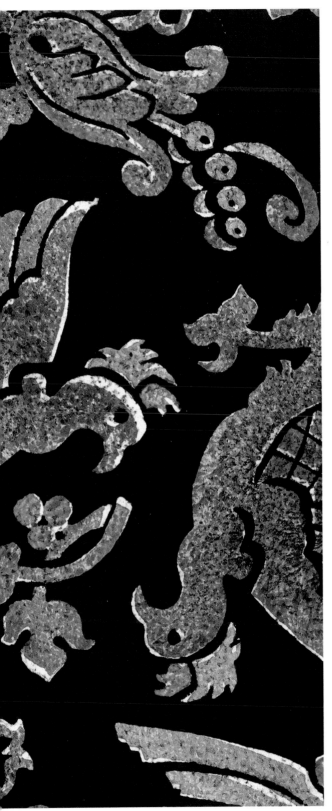

History also can provide interesting themes. Often, periods or movements are in fashion. Both the thirties, known as Art Deco, and the fifties styles have enjoyed revivals. Information on both these eras can be found in many books and museums.

Art Deco is typified by certain colour combinations, such as black and white, pale pink and green and pink and grey, as well as by strong geometric design imagery. Art Deco designs came in various sizes, from small-scale, repeating motifs to large-scale, geometric patterns.

The fifties, on the other hand, was less conventional in its imagery, with strange 'sputnik'-shaped motifs in primary colours, and organic shapes abstracted to create unusual patterns for furnishing fabrics. Often the period is referred to as a time of bad taste, of kitsch, but some of the more unusual and amusing characteristics of the time could be used to good effect (see page 83).

Another ever-popular period is the Victorian era. Heavily patterned furnishings and screens, with ornate curtains or blinds in rich colours, could create a nineteenth-century atmosphere in your own home. Furnishing fabrics produced during the early Victorian period were elaborately patterned, often featuring repeating motifs of exotic birds and florals.

Fabrics from this period would be difficult to produce on the kitchen table today, but they are a marvellous source of inspiration. An elaborately stencilled border using birds, leaves and flowers could, for example, be co-ordinated with a bought furnishing fabric reminiscent of the period. The very full look of Victorian designs can be achieved by using a mixture of hand-painted and machine-patterned fabric. Hand paint motifs on bought fabrics, and for added authenticity use tassels and fringes to finish the edges. Bright, almost garish colours were often used in fabric designs of the period using realistically printed florals (see pages 13-15).

50s style print
Jasia Szerszynska has drawn her inspiration from 50s motifs and colourways for this hand painted and printed fabric.

ETHNIC THEMES

An 'ethnic' style is relatively easy to create by using stencils on furniture as well as on fabric. Use soft or primary colours in simple, almost naive patterns. Inspiration for these can be found by looking at the characteristic styles and cultures of other countries and peoples such as the North American Indians and mid-Europeans.

European farming communities of the sixteenth century had a discernible culture of their own. Although their symbols and motifs had a naive quality about them, they tended to represent things of great significance, such as fertility and the harvest. The motifs were often drawn from nature and their use of bright colours produced exquisite patterns. Many of their designs were painted freehand or richly embroidered in vivid colours.

Blue and white is a popular colour theme throughout Africa, often rendered in the shape of simple checks and stripes. An indigo dye is used to achieve the many shades of blue. Indigo dye is extracted from plants and is one of the oldest dyes known. Many of the patterns were created by methods known to us as tie and dye and batik. These types of design can easily be interpreted using commercial dyes on calicoes and cottons.

Pattern and border
Miroslava hand blocked this fabric using two designs. The border of faces gives the cushion fabric an ethnic feel.

American Indians developed a highly stylized form of pattern and colour. Their patterns symbolized the elements of their surroundings and the colours represented the water, sky and earth. The rich, almost startling, colours associated with Indian fabrics

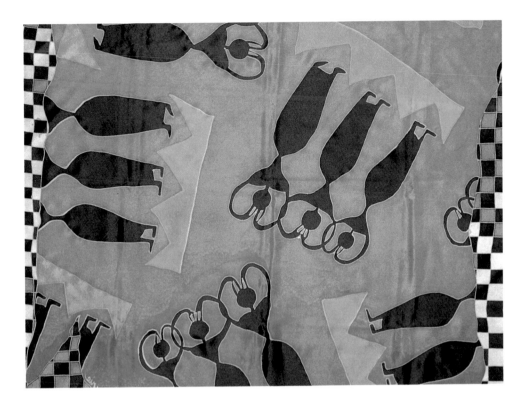

always include black, black with red, yellow and shades of brown. Navajo rugs use a variety of simple geometric shapes, each one representing canyons, plateaus and earth. Although the rugs are woven, the colours and simple patterns lend themselves beautifully to painted and printed fabric techniques. The shapes are particularly easy to translate on to cloth. Once cut out, the shapes could be stencilled, screen printed or simply hand painted. Ideally, you should endeavour to use the same colour combinations, and these should be mixed and tested on scrap fabric beforehand.

Moving on to South America, primitive motifs are found in abundance, and the imagery reflects the world around the artist – birds, flowers, the sun and wheels, are very common. As with other tropical areas, the colours used are very bright, almost fluorescent. A mixture of sizzling colours and motifs are usually all brought together in the same design. Children's drawings, painted in dazzlingly bright colours, would be representative of South American decoration.

Remember, some of these ideas and themes require very little skill, just patience, enthusiasm and the desire to experiment. There is economy in this approach, too, for by choosing simple, pleasing designs, you will be less inclined to chop and change and perhaps start all over again.

African theme
The colours and images used by Frannie in this hand-painted design echo African cloth.

FABRICS FOR
WINDOWS

Windows are the eyes of a room. The way in
which they are dressed, and the types of
colours, patterns, designs and motifs used, all
have an immense impact and, therefore, need
to be considered as part of the overall decor.
And not only do you need to consider how the
windows look from the inside, you must also
bear in mind the type of effect you are
creating when they are viewed from the
outside, as part of the facade of your home.
The choice of styles at your disposal is
immense, ranging from the uncompromising
flat surfaces of roller blinds through to the
ruffles and frills of curtains and highly ornate
Austrian and festoon blinds. Every type of
surface and material used is a unique
opportunity to make a statement about your
lifestyle, and a chance to complement and
enhance the environment in each individual
room. This chapter helps you to make the right
choice for your scheme.

DECIDING ON A STYLE

Fabrics for windows are an integral part of interior design. No longer do we have such a limited choice in what is acceptable as window covering. Curtains can suggest fabrics knotted, tied, pinned, draped, held back with bows or gathered. Anything goes as long as it enhances the rest of the decor. Since windows usually cover a sizeable area of the available wall space, they are ideal for painted fabric projects, and some fabric paints, such as silk paints, look even more impressive with light shining through them.

The drapes and folds of curtains, whether they are a sheer voile or a heavy canvas, add a new dimension to a static design. Before any decisions are made about the design and fabric, though, consider the final effect. Traditional interiors may call for a classic design, perhaps a stencil motif on a luxurious fabric, hung so that it falls in folds. For a more feminine, softer style, try painted old lace, or pastel-sponged voile, both of which filter light entering the room. But for a very contemporary look, consider a textured or geometric design in strong, bright colours painted on to a roller blind or a large area of heavy cotton or canvas. These types of design make a strong statement in an otherwise plain room.

Roller blinds lend themselves to scenes or to *trompe-l'oeil* effects, often used to best advantage in a kitchen or a child's bedroom. Festoon blinds or Austrian blinds, on the other hand,

Chalky effects
The designer chose a subtle blend of colours and used casual brush-strokes to achieve the desired effect. The chalky look of the paint was acquired by adding colour to white.

Mural blind
The seventeenth-century mural painters provided Althea Wilson with the inspiration for this hand-painted Roman blind (shown closed on page 58). She used emulsion paint to evoke the solidity of a painted wall.

Border for a blind
The design from the curtain braid was hand painted onto the blind to create a simple but effective co-ordinating border.

may be better suited to a textured design or sponged effect. A painted fabric need not necessarily have been painted specifically for a window. A hand-painted piece of silk, for example, may have originally been painted for a dress fabric or a piece of furniture, but if hung at a window in the appropriate setting it could look marvellous.

How the fabric is hung can make the design more exciting and powerful, and sometimes the simplest ideas work best. It may look just right, for example, thrown over a pole or gathered in the

Austrian blind
Blind Alley hand painted a
random design onto soft
fabric. When ruched, the
fabric changes as the folds
distort the original pattern.

middle. Have fun trying out all these ideas. After all, windows do
not have to be treated with two lengths of plain fabric that meet
in the middle.

PLANNING AND DESIGNING

When thinking about painted fabrics, consider the proportions of
the room, since colour and style can modify all kinds of mistakes
and problems. Your design can, for example, create a sense of
height and space in a small room, or a more intimate atmosphere in a large room. Remember, a window tends to be a focal
point, so plan the design and colour carefully.

A small window can be just as challenging as elaborate
drapes for large windows. Also, conventional curtains may not
be what you want or they may not be appropriate for a variety of
architectural reasons. The style and shape of the furniture may
well influence your design – you may want to use curved or
linear patterns to relate to the shape of the sofa, for example.
The space within a room will determine whether a bold design is
called for, or a simple, small-scale design to soften the impact of
the other elements there.

The colours of your design will have an effect on the whole
room, so it is important that you spend time planning colour,
fabric and the actual design within the context of that room.
Consider the amount of colour to be used; too much and the end
result will be overpowering; too little and it will be insipid.
Ensure, too, that the fabric is suitable for the design and that it is
not too sheer or too textured.

All of these considerations also apply to your choice of win-

Roller blind mural
Blind Alley used hand
painting and auto sprays to
create this *trompe l'oeil*
effect.

Florals and stripes
Julia Fieldwick hand painted silk (see page 136) for these swagged floral curtains. She used the main motif's colours for the striped tie-backs, and trimmed them with striped rosettes that echo the painted flower shape.

dow covering. Roller blinds can be painted after they have been bought ready-made, but other types of blinds and curtains must be painted before they are made up. Consideration must also be given to where seams will lie if they are not to break up a vital motif. How will the design look when pleated, ruched and folded? Practice on small pieces of the fabric, and try folding and pleating them to see how the design distorts and if any of the colours disappear.

Ruching and pleating take up a lot of fabric, so think about the space available to work in. If there is not sufficient to complete the design comfortably, try painting it outside (weather permitting) or consider a more manageable design or just a border as an alternative.

It is a good idea to paint a section of the design first and hang it up at the window. This will give you a chance to look at it from a distance. In context, it may look totally different – too pale, too dark, too simple or too complex. Now is the time to make changes and rectify any mistakes.

Once you are satisfied that you have covered all of these points, map out the design. Keep the motifs to scale and have enough paint mixed to complete the piece. For a large area of regular, repeating design, you might need to measure distances between motifs to make sure that they are evenly spaced and that the balance of the design looks right.

HAND-DECORATED BLINDS

Roller blinds can be bought ready-made or in kit form to be used in conjunction with the fabric of your choice. However, the fabric used for blinds needs to be stiff (called Holland; see page 152) so that it hangs flat and straight and does not crease. Kits sometimes contain fabric stiffener, or this can be bought separately.

Once the design has been worked out to your satisfaction, draw it up to scale on paper exactly the same size as the fabric for the blind. Bear in mind that a design often can look acceptable when small, but once motifs are enlarged they may not work as well. These problems can be seen easily and remedied on paper.

Colours, too, should be worked out at this stage. As with the scale of the motifs, what may look like the appropriate amount of black could be totally overpowering when the design is enlarged. If you cannot match exactly the colours used on your paper pattern to those for the fabric, don't worry. Just use the nearest shades to give an impression of the finished effect.

If you are painting on to fabric that will later be made into a blind, remember to allow for fabric at the top and bottom. It could be disastrous if an integral part of the design is hemmed at the bottom and rolled at the top. Blind kits always state how much fabric to leave unpainted top and bottom, so always read the instructions carefully.

When all these criteria are satisfied, transfer the design on to your fabric, using tailor's chalk. Blinds are not washed, so pencil will leave a mark.

If there is a fairly large, flat area for painting, use the appropriate size brush. Painting flat areas of colour on to a ready-made blind can be quite difficult, unless it is a roller blind, so spread out the paint in even strokes. It will probably be necessary to paint a second coat, but let the first one dry first.

Blinds are coated with a layer of a plastic-like substance to help them retain their stiffness, so fixing has to be carried out carefully. Ironing the fabric is the usual way of fixing, but in this case it is not to be recommended. Instead, you should fix the colours using a hairdryer, set to hot, for a few minutes on each area of fabric.

Even though blinds are not washed, damp caused by condensation can have a disastrous effect on your design, making the colours run and bleed. If damp is a particular problem, consider using auto spray or acrylic paint, which have the added advan-

Timney-Fowler detail
This close-up shows a classical motif that is typical of the designers' work. Such a screen-printed motif would be repeated many times over on a fabric.

Classical influence
Motifs inspired by ancient Greece are strengthened by a black outline. Annie Doherty hand printed this fabric.

tage of stiffening the fabric still further. (This makes them totally unsuitable for use with ordinary cottons and silks rather than Holland.) Auto spray paints do not need to be fixed and they give a good, even coverage. However, care is necessary when using these spray cans. You will need plenty of space and make sure you cover all nearby surfaces. If there are any straight lines on your design, stick masking tape to the fabric and paint or spray between the strips. Leave the paint to dry before removing the tape. If you are spraying, make sure that the rest of the blind is protected from drifting paint.

Designer blind and curtains
Julia Fieldwick created this unique window treatment by hand printing the frilled curtain edges and pelmet, along with the tie-backs. She used a simple geometric design to colour co-ordinate with the Austrian blind.

Whatever paint you use, if it has been properly fixed, you should not experience any problems with sunlight fading the colours of your design.

PAINTING BEFORE MAKING UP
Festoon, Roman and Austrian blinds must be painted before being made up. The design that might look perfect on a flat roller blind could look very confusing on ruched and pleated blinds. So planning and designing for these is more complicated.

Perhaps simple checks or stripes or random coloured dashes

would look effective on these types of blind. The shapes will distort when gathered, but if the designs are simple, then this might add to the effect. During the day these types of blind are usually gathered half-way up, so additional interest is created in seeing the design as it was painted and then distorted. When you paint on to fabric before it is sewn, always take into consideration seam allowances and fix the design before sewing.

CO-ORDINATING CURTAINS, PELMETS AND TIE-BACKS

Tie-backs and pelmets constitute a much smaller area to work on than curtains or blinds. A more complicated design could be attempted on them, which would be too time-consuming or just too difficult to attempt on a larger area. This could be the starting point for a complete co-ordinated effect throughout a room. The curtains, for example, could be plain, therefore the interest would be created by the decorated pelmet and tie-backs, which could be hand painted or printed in bold contrast to the plain fabric and so become a prominent feature.

If you are painting fabric for the first time, working on an area sufficient for curtains can be nerve-wracking. This is understandable as even the most experienced fabric designers get a touch of nerves when starting on a vast area of fabric. At your first attempt, perhaps a simple block-printed geometric shape or spot could be tried on the curtains, using just a single colour, and then this co-ordinated with a much more elaborate, multicoloured geometric pattern on the pelmet and tie-backs. Parts of the design on the curtain could be emphasized by painting the same motifs, but in a different colour, on the tie-backs and pelmet. Alternatively, the curtain motif could be used as a border along the pelmet.

Imaginative use of colour could create interest where there is only one design motif. For example, if the curtains are painted with black spots on a white background the tie-backs could be white spots on black. Just by changing the applied colour or the fabric background you can create a very pleasing contrast. For an effective example of this, look at Celia Birtwell's curtain fabrics on pages 68-9.

An extremely effective technique if you are using sheer or semi-sheer fabric, is to try to match the colour of the paint to that of the fabric to add a translucent quality to your design. If the fabric is a fine jap silk or a cotton voile (see pages 26-7) in white, for example, then use white fabric paint. The effect will be quite subtle but nevertheless striking.

Jungle tie-back
The densely filled jungle paintings of Henri Rousseau gave Gill Dickinson the idea for this small area of hand-painted fabric. As a curtain tie-back it is a perfect foil for the large expanse of plain fabric.

Stencilled tie-back
The fabric for this tie-back was hand stencilled using a spray paint (see pages 132 and 155), then cut to follow the edge of the design and padded to form a three-dimensional tie.

67

CO-ORDINATING WITH EXISTING FURNISHING

Any new addition to a room needs to complement the overall scheme, but it is possible to introduce new designs with the existing decor in mind. The easiest approach here is to take the major design motifs within the room, perhaps from the carpet, wallpaper or duvet. Then, simply by picking up on a shape or colour, you will have the basis for a co-ordinated, entirely original, design. This repeated motif may be enlarged to quite a grand scale for use on a blind or curtains, or it may be repeated on a smaller scale and in many colours over a large area. Even a section of a design from a complicated carpet or rug can be enlarged on to a piece of fabric. Any of these ideas could be stencilled (see page 134) or screen printed (see page 144). This way, you can liven up the interior without going to the expense of completely redecorating.

This approach is experimental, but start by looking at the individual designs carefully and trying out existing design elements. Distort conventional shapes or use unusual colour combinations, and experiment with different combinations of shapes – reduced, enlarged, textured or flat. Practise on paper as well as on scraps of fabric while thinking of the most appropriate painting or printing technique for this new design. Choose the most eye-catching features and colours of the design and use these as your starting point.

Painted walls, such as those featuring murals, often require a co-ordinating window covering if continuity is not to be lost. So, continue the theme by painting on to a blind or curtain a scene inspired by the mural. These days there are many painted wall effects, any of which can be copied on to fabric in either harmonizing or contrasting colours.

In a particular room, perhaps the only pattern is on the rug. Use this design and transfer it to the blind or curtain fabric, again considering whether the same or a contrasting colour scheme should be used.

Random snatches of existing patterning worked into your design are often all that is needed to link old and new furnishings. Sometimes there is a focal point to a room other than the furnishings – a fireplace, for example, or a painted piece of china. Use these objects to inspire a new and totally original design that will tie together the existing decor. Another useful aspect of this approach is its cost-saving qualities. For example, if you have just made two rooms into one, rather than replace the curtains at both ends of the new room you could adapt a motif from the largest set to make co-ordinating curtains for the smaller windows.

White on white
The combination of opaque, white pigment and other fabric is particularly effective used as a window covering. Natural light shining through emphasizes the dense shape of the motif.

Traditional paisley
The same, simple paisley motif has been used by Celia Birtwell on two different fabric types to produce a complementary effect. The main curtain is hand-screen-printed cotton (see p. 144), while the other is sheer fabric printed with white.

FABRICS FOR
FURNITURE

All furniture benefits from the softening effect of fabrics, whether it is in the form of loose covers on a sofa or cushions on a chair. Fabrics provide both comfort and style; interiors without any decorative surfaces tend to look cold and uninviting.

This chapter shows you the different ways you can use hand decorated fabric to enhance your furniture. You need not stick rigidly to one pattern or style; try a softer setting where a variety of styles, patterns and shapes can be mixed together. Just as traditional styles of furniture can be teamed with contemporary fabric designs and complement each other, so too can modern furniture be compatible with fabrics featuring traditional motifs such as stencilled florals.

CO·ORDINATION

Upholstery fabric can be decorated to co-ordinate with the rest of the piece. For example, you could apply a painted effect such as spattering (see page 130) to a chair frame and carry through the same technique onto the upholstery fabric.

There are also many ways that fabrics can be used to link furniture with the rest of the room scheme. For example, you may like to use the same fabric for curtains and sofa upholstery, or pick up the motifs from the curtains and wall-paper and apply them both to a chair.

In bedrooms the use of similar themes on both curtain fabric and bed covers and upholstery can produce very cosy, romantic or even dramatic looks.

Classic cane
Annie Doherty's length of fabric, with its modern use of classical imagery, is teamed here with a cane sofa and hand-painted silk cushions by Penny Beard. The black outlines were laid down first, then tones of one colour were used to fill in (see p. 136).

SCREENS

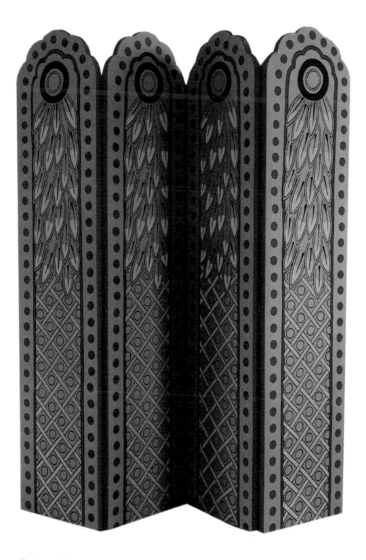

Geometric screen
Cressida Bell hand printed the fabric for this attractive screen. The heraldic patterns suit the shaped Gothic top of the frame.

Painted fabric screens are an unusual and original way to add decoration to a living room or bedroom. Although widely used in the past, especially in the Victorian era and the Art Nouveau period, today they are usually only available as antiques or as one-offs by designer/craftsmen and at a fairly high price. A hand-painted screen can make a valuable contribution to your home and it can be an effective and functional alternative to a painting or a print.

A screen consists of two, three or more panels, hinged together into a row, with the fabric stretched between each panel. A softwood, such as pine, is fine for the framework, which can either be incorporated into the design or the fabric stretched over it to hide it completely.

When designing fabric for a screen, decide whether to treat each panel separately, with some kind of colour scheme used to

co-ordinate and link them, or to design one pattern to cover all the panels. The design will still have to be drawn on to a piece of fabric for each panel, whether each panel matches or not. If one design is spread over all the panels, make sure the design motifs match up from panel to panel.

To do this, draw the full-size design on paper and only transfer the design to the fabric using tailor's chalk when you are satisfied with the motifs. If the design works well over the whole area, place the pieces of fabric together and start to paint a section at a time. If the design is an abstract or geometric pattern with large areas of flat colour, use a heavy canvas or cotton fabric. Since your screen will constitute quite a large area of fabric that cannot be washed, artist's acrylic paints or auto spray paints may be more suitable to use than standard fabric paints (see pages 153-5).

Co-ordinating furniture
Sarah Collins hand painted and printed fabric to cover this chair and screen. The designs are not identical, but the common style and colours give the pieces a harmonious look.

Gather together the appropriate brushes and masking tape, which is used to block out areas not to be painted and to define any straight edges and stripes. If the screen fabric is silk, you could look to traditional design sources, such as Japanese or Chinese silk paintings or Art Deco imagery for inspiration. If the screen is for a bedroom then perhaps stencilled motifs would be suitable. Alternatively, if the screen is going to be positioned in a room with good natural light, a design incorporating the gutta resist method (see page 136) with silk paints could look beautiful when backlit.

Combining fabrics with furniture
Fabrics can be combined with metal as well as wood. Carolyn Quartermaine used a specially designed wrought iron frame for this unique hand-painted fabric screen.

Although the hand painted or printed screen will not be washed or cleaned once it is attached to its frame, if you are using any type of fabric paint rather than auto spray paint you must fix the colours as carefully as possible. Damp and condensation can affect the fabric paint, causing it to bleed, and light can fade the design all too quickly.

CHAIRS AND SOFAS

Throwover for a sofa
A simple hand-painted check design in soft colours echoes the floor pattern and the paint effect on the walls. This treatment is ideal for a restrained room scheme.

Co-ordinating fabrics with painted furniture is just an extension of matching fabrics in a room, and the flexibility of the techniques means that fabrics can be painted to match any kind of patterned surface, such as a vase or carpet. Also, you can simplify the pattern or reduce the number of colours used if this will be easier to paint.

A hand-painted piece of silk could be used loosely draped at a window or thrown over a sofa. If, however, the fabric is to co-ordinate with a painted chair, it may instead take the form of a cushion or, again, just be draped across the back or arms of the chair. Obviously, the paint used for the chair will differ from that used for fabric. Note that fabric paint cannot be used for any other surface, but fabric paints can be mixed to match virtually any colour. Try out different colourways of the design on scraps of fabric and place them on the chair to see how they look. The design used on the wood, but painted onto the fabric in another colourway, would make the chair more interesting.

Painted furniture can be used in any room, and the appropriate fabrics can be painted to suit both the furniture and its setting. A set of old dining chairs, for example, painted in bright colours, could be teamed with a hand-painted tablecloth picking up the colours from the chairs.

Stencilling is a popular decorative finish for painted furniture and it is widely used to co-ordinate fabrics, walls and furniture. You will have to match up colours in different paint types: fabric paint for curtains, water-based emulsion for walls and oil-based paint for furniture.

Geometric throw
This vividly coloured hand-printed throw by Anna Tilson would brighten a plain sofa. Or drape it over a table, with a plain cloth beneath.

REVAMPING OLD FURNITURE

Antique and upholstered furniture in a dilapidated condition can be expensive to repair and often the cost far outweighs the value of the piece. Now you can revamp this furniture by painting it and then adding hand-painted fabric. For a unique and unusual effect use a contemporary design, such as a multicoloured stipple, as a contrast to a traditional piece. Many types of upholstered armchairs have some kind of exposed wooden frame which can also be incorporated into your design.

If the upholstery is plain fabric, you can paint directly on to it. It might take a little while to dry, but this process can be speeded up with the use of a hairdryer. For the multicoloured stipple effect on both the frame and the fabric, first mix a selection of primary-coloured fabric paints. Then use a 2.5 cm (1 in) brush dipped into the paint to add small dashes all over the surface. Overlap the colours to cover most of the background, and keep the colours bright and fresh by washing out the brush, or

Tied-up crocodiles
You have to look carefully to appreciate fully this clever design, in which gift-wrapped crocodiles snap at each other's tails.

using a new one, each time you change colours. Now, using the appropriate paint, continue the design on to the frame using exactly the same colours. This kind of design could look marvellous on an old, but once elaborate, chair – for example, try replacing gilt and velvet with a painted contemporary pattern.

The traditional use of painting techniques for furniture can be used in a contemporary way on a piece of old furniture by spattering, spraying and sponging the wood. (see pages 127-31). Continue the same pattern on to the fabric, which could be draped or thrown casually over the piece.

Upholstered fabric is fixed firmly in place and cannot be removed for washing. Unless you are painting on the existing upholstery, you must use a replacement fabric that is strong and hard wearing, and then fix the fabric paint using heat (see page 155) before having the chair upholstered.

Many modern pieces of furniture have been inspired by the past and, therefore, incorporate traditional shapes, fabrics and

Designed with humour
The hand-screen-printed cotton (see p. 144) by Pazuki Prints is in a traditional colourway and has an obvious repeat, but the amusing design makes it highly distinctive and original.

woods, or they have successfully combined traditional imagery with modern materials. Fabrics for these pieces can be designed in exactly the same way. Large-scale furniture combined with distressed timbers and steel could look overpowering without fabric to soften the hard lines, and black and white geometrics or pastel florals could suit the pieces very well. Lighter pieces of furniture that use decorative metal could be enhanced by a soft abstract design painted on to a sheer or fine silk fabric.

Use your imagination when choosing colours for different styles of furniture. If the furniture is heavy, use colours and fabrics to lighten the effect. Don't think that heavy wood finishes

Vamping up plain covers
A plain bought sofa cover was enhanced with a simple one-colour motif. A dry household paint brush was dipped in white fabric paint and drawn across the cloth in one even stroke.

need to have colours and fabrics in a similar style: this will only create a solid, dull appearance. The same principle applies to very modern furniture. For a more attractive and comfortable look, use soft colours and shapes and luxurious fabrics rather than paint a very hard geometric pattern in strong colours.

If the furniture has any decorative elements, perhaps these could be incorporated into the design of the fabric. The motifs could be traced or copied from the furniture and used actual size if they are not too large. Alternatively, you could use just one motif painted and repeated all over the fabric or one image combined with a textured background. Another idea is to pair the furniture motif together with a motif from another fabric used in the

same room and combine them to decorate the fabric. As with all fabric painting, experiment on paper to start with, combining shapes, textures and colours, and then move on to the fabric only when you are happy that the design works well in the room as well as on the furniture.

LOOSE COVERS

Most styles of armchair and sofa look attractive with loose covers, and they can be removed easily for cleaning. Whether your covers are new or old, they will almost certainly be suitable for painting.

Old, worn loose covers in a plain-coloured fabric can be given a new lease of life by applying an appropriate painting technique to them. Since these covers are already made up, select your design carefully to accommodate all the stitched corners and odd angles. For example, a large-scale design with shapes that fit together would be too difficult to paint, but a textured pattern or a random spot motif could be successful, as could stripes, dashes and stipples.

If the only decorative surface in the room is the sofa cover, then obviously it does not need to co-ordinate. In this type of situation, the sofa cover will be the focal point of the room, whether it is a multicoloured design or a classic motif painted in subtle shades.

COPING WITH MADE-UP COVERS

To paint made-up loose covers, first remove them from the sofa and place them on a flat surface. To prevent paint seeping through, insert paper or polythene between the cushion covers and where the main cover has to be folded. If possible, try and overlap the design to cover the sides of the seat covers and thus give a more cohesive look.

The rest of the cover will be more difficult to paint because it is already stitched and it is therefore an awkward shape. The best approach is to paint it in sections, and keep moving the fabric round while you paint over the seams so that no obvious gaps appear once the cover is back on the sofa.

STARTING FROM SCRATCH

If you are making up your own loose covers, you should paint the fabric before sewing. But whether the cloth should be painted before or after it has been cut out will depend on the design. If the same one or two motifs are to be stencilled, printed or painted all over the ground, then paint the fabric before cutting it out. However, if the design is more complex, with different

Matching fabric to walls
Special paint effects used on the walls can be extended onto matching soft furnishings. Here, geometrics in neutral shades are hand painted on a loose cover and used as a wall mural.

Fabric detail
This hand-printed design by Sara Robbins would make an attractive throw for a sofa, but the pattern is too 'square' for loose covers.

shapes fitting together, then cut out the fabric first and paint the design on the individual pieces. This is particularly necessary if the design is one-directional or on a large scale.

Choice of fabric is an important consideration, and because of the hard wear loose covers are subjected to, always buy the best quality you can afford. It is not worth going to all this trouble only to find that your fabric is looking tatty within six months! The fabric should be tough, hard wearing and non-shrinkable, wherever possible.

THROW-OVERS

An instant transformation for an old sofa can be brought about by covering it with fabric that is literally thrown over without any sewing whatsoever. There are several ways this can be done. Either paint sufficient fabric to cover the back of the sofa or use a few differently painted fabrics on the sofa, overlapping them so that the designs or patterns provide an attractive patchwork effect. For a more cohesive look, use one piece of fabric that will cover the entire length of the sofa. These simple ideas for recovering furniture will also show off the hand-painted designs to best advantage, which have been made all the easier to paint by not having corners, seams or any awkward angles to cope with.

Whatever the style of design or type of fabric, the fabric paint has to be fixed in order to make the design permanent so that it can be washed or dry-cleaned.

FIXED COVERS

Painting or printing textiles for furniture needs more consideration than a spontaneous effect on a curtain length. If the cloth is to be attached permanently to a piece of furniture – an expensive, time-consuming process – then time has to be spent considering the design, the fabric and the method to be employed. A good-quality material has to be used (one that will last and wear well), as there is no point investing time or money attaching the fabric, only to find it wearing out after a short time. Deciding on the right sort of design to be printed or painted is as important as the material you use; not only must it be suitable for the fabric, it must also fit in with the piece of furniture and the surrounding decor. You should plan the design carefully before you start – it may have to be painted in sections and then fitted together when the cover is attached permanently.

When thinking of permanent coverings most of us think of upholstered chairs, but screens (see page 73), chests, occasional and dressing tables can have fabric as permanent coverings too. Dressing tables are often covered with a mass-

Fabric-covered dressing table
Yvonne Chambers hand painted this circus design with a brushstroke technique, and used it to cover a kidney-shaped dressing table. For a detail of the fabric design see page 24.

produced fabric. There is no reason why this cloth cannot be hand-painted to individualize the piece and fit it in to an existing colour scheme. The fabric on a bought table is usually ruched or pleated, so choose an all-over pattern in a small geometric or a painted effect – this way the pattern will not be hidden. If a soft pastel look is required, a sponged fabric in shades of one colour or a range of pastel colours would look pretty. The same technique could be used for a fabric-covered table. As the design is all-over, there is no need to worry about matching the patterns at seams and joins. However, if a more ambitious pattern is required, the design will have to be worked out carefully on the fabric, once it has been cut-out to fit the table and before it has been glued.

First home
The 50s style hand painted fabric by Jasia Szerszynska is ideal for this instant low-budget scheme. When more furnishings arrive, the fabric could be used for cushions.

DECKCHAIRS

Most deckchairs use striped canvas and after a time this will need renewing. So why not use a plain-coloured canvas and add an appropriate design before fixing the canvas back on to its frame? The frame could also be painted to match the fabric design if you wish.

Deckchairs are very informal and, therefore, lend themselves to bold designs in bright colours, such as simple wavy lines in primaries or large geometrics with a brightly coloured frame. Whatever the design, draw it out on paper first to actual size. Use your intended colours, too, since this is the only way to tell whether the design is what you really want. Play around with shapes; cut them out and move them around until the best arrangement is found. A simple wavy line design could work by

Hand-painted deckchair
Bold hand-painted shapes like these are easy to carry out, as described on this page. This would be an ideal project for a beginner.

painting the lines closer together at the bottom of the canvas, spacing them out more towards the top. This is only a simple change, but it is one that could make the design look that bit more thoughtful.

To give a better impression of how the design will eventually look, cut out the shapes from coloured paper and position them on the plain canvas, rather like a collage. The subject matter sets the design style so there are some limitations. Another design idea is to use a theme. Obvious ones are often the best, such as the beach or the sea, using the imagery connected with both these subjects. Approached in an original way, perhaps more abstract than realistic, these images could work well on this type of chair. Motifs could be either hand painted or stencilled (see page 132).

Director's chair
This hand-painted fabric by Fanny Wilder makes an attractive cover for an indoor chair. The fabric was simply painted with a decorator's foam roller. Attaching the cover is easy too, so this would make an ideal beginner's project.

TYPES OF CANVAS AND PAINT

Deckchair canvas is made to a standard width to just fit the deckchair frame, therefore the sides do not have to be considered. Do, however, allow enough fabric to be attached to the top and bottom of the frame. Obviously, deckchair canvas has to be strong and hard-wearing. This means that the fabric will absorb quite a lot of paint, so make sure you mix sufficient of each colour to apply at least two coats of fabric paint to guarantee even coverage. Use tailor's chalk to draw the design on to the canvas. Pencil can be used, but as the deckchair cover will not be washed too often, pencil will leave a mark.

Make sure the painted design is fixed properly before attaching the canvas to the frame. Although frequent washing is unlikely, damp or rainwater will cause the design to run.

An alternative medium to consider is auto spray paint, which is permanent as soon as it dries. Since canvas is thick, such paint gives excellent coverage, but remember to mask out all the other areas of canvas (and cover all nearby surrounding surfaces) when spraying to protect them from drifting paint.

Hold the spray can 15-30 cm (6-12 in) away from the fabric and, with a sideways stroking motion back and forth, spray until the desired coverage is achieved. Allow a few seconds between each pass to avoid a build-up of excess paint.

SOFT

FURNISHINGS

This chapter is all about how to exploit the colours, textures and patterns of cloth, and the ways different hand painted and printed fabrics can be put together to create the most appealing decorative scheme. You will see here how, for example, large-scale patterns can work with small-scale ones, and how you can use different colour combinations to provide interest in any room in the house. Whether you plan to decorate fabrics to cover the main features of a room – a duvet cover for a bedroom, for example – or would prefer to start simply by painting a set of linen napkins, you will be making an original addition to your home.

CUSHION COVERS

Soft Art
Cushions are on a small enough scale to merit more elaborate painting. Penny Beard's witty Venus, hand-painted on silk (see page 138), shows the possibilities cushions offer to the more experienced fabric painter.

Cushion covers seem to be a popular starting point for most fabric painters. Although a cushion is a relatively small area to paint, there is unlimited scope in the choice of fabric and design. And, as well as adding the finishing touches to sofas, chairs, beds and so on, cushions provide extra interest in both shape and design. Also, painting cushion covers can often give you the confidence you need to tackle more ambitious projects for other parts of your home.

Almost any fabric is suitable for cushions, therefore virtually any decorating technique can be employed, and ready made edgings and trimmings can be added afterwards if necessary. A printed geometric design, for example, could look all the more professional with a contrasting piped edge, while a soft-coloured, stencilled cushion could be enhanced by the addition of a lace edging. Consider hand painting home-made or bought piping or cord too, to co-ordinate with your design. Or carry your design around a scalloped or pointed cloth edge. And there are many decorative sewing techniques you can combine with hand colouring to create an exclusive cushion – think about using quilting, embroidery, buttoning or ribbonwork.

Your imagination can run riot; cushions can be any size or shape you want and designs do not necessarily have to co-ordinate. When you get bored with a certain arrangement, simply move them to a new position or a different room. Elaborately painted cushions often work well when contrasted with plain ones, so it is worth trying out ambitious designs since they always produce an individual focal point in a room setting.

Matching cushions to curtains
Simple screen printed shapes (see page 144) are very effective for co-ordinated soft furnishings. For maximum impact, keep to the same colour range.

Co-ordinated cushions
Here, Anna Tilson uses the same colour range on a series of cushions so that her strong screen printed (see page 144) designs, which might otherwise conflict, work well together.

Bought cushion covers, whether old or new, can easily be painted as long as the manufacturer's finish is removed before starting. And you should always remember to place paper between the back and the front of the cover before starting work to prevent any paint seeping through to the cushion back while you are working.

Fruit and leaves
Diluted fabric paints were used to achieve a soft, watercolour effect on these cushions.

DESIGN ADVICE

Silk cushions may demand a more formal approach to design. A simple floral motif, for example, or a bow stencilled in one corner in pastel colours, may be just enough to work with the existing decor of your room. Florals, bows and ribbons can all be traced or copied from books or existing fabrics and do not represent a particular problem. Make sure, though, that the size of the motif fits well into the area of cushion cover you have allowed for it, whether it is the corner or the centre. Just place the motif (drawn on paper) on to the cushion cover and move it around until you are satisfied with its position. The design can then be transferred by pencil on to the fabric or, if stencilling, the stencil can be cut (see page 132).

Special silk paints used on silk fabrics (see page 136) are ideal for certain types of imagery; the effect will be like a watercolour, with soft edges and merging colours.

Florals are the most difficult motifs to produce, especially if you are trying to paint a realistic looking flower. Initially, try painting simple floral shapes in tones of one colour. Alternatively, use opaque fabric paint and a very dry brush and paint dry brush strokes in the shape of petals. Create highlights with lighter shades of paint, and dots and dashes can be added to

Cushions
Julia Fieldwick's hand painted cushions soften the severe lines of this Victorian chaise longue. If you stick to harmonious shades, you can mix patterns and techniques very successfully.

give more variety to your design. These techniques will be more effective and the finish more professional than if you try to paint too realistically – unless you are really proficient.

If you are making your own cushions, cut out the fabric first and then paint the pieces before assembling them. Remember to allow sufficient fabric for the seams so that none of your design disappears into the joins.

Consider designing cushions to co-ordinate with a painted or stencilled bedspread. Experienced seamstresses could add embroidery or quilting to the cushions to give added definition to the painted motif and provide a visual link to the bedspread (see page 98). Or, cushions could be designed as a non-identical group. For example, a group of floor cushions, either for a living area or a children's room, could have contrasting geometric designs painted on them, together with varying painted effects in the same bold, brilliant colours.

Cave paintings
A hand-painted and printed design by Penny Beard, which was based on prehistoric cave paintings. The background has been painted to add more texture to the fabric and to give it a 'rock-like' appearance.

BED·LINEN

Plain cotton sheets and duvet covers which have lost their colour after constant washing, can be revived to their former glory by dyeing. The easiest and most permanent method is to use a washing machine and the correctly formulated dye and fix (see page 150).

Most commercial dyes are meant for use with natural fabrics, and therefore if your bed-linen is a mixture of man-made and natural fibres the results will be paler than the colour shown on the packet. By dyeing linen plain colours, you make a feature of the colour itself. If you want a bold effect every item – from pillow to duvet cover – can be dyed in a different primary colour, an idea that is particularly popular with children.

White bed-linen that has gone grey with constant use and washing could be transformed into a matching pastel set or, for a more masculine look, consider the less delicate colours of grey and black. The same principle can be applied to towels. Dull, faded towels take dye beautifully, and the colours can be quite brilliant and perfectly fast. Towels are not, however, suitable for painting, since the surface of towelling is too textured to allow the paint to adhere properly. Also, towels spend too much time wet or damp and after a short time the fabric paint will start to flake off and look patchy.

Dyed backgrounds can also be painted. A multicoloured spatter effect (see page 130) teamed with a sprayed (see page 128) or

Co-ordinating pillows
These pillows by Carolyn Quartermaine are hand painted. The Egyptian design co-ordinates with the duvet shown on pages 94-5. As an alternative to motifs or patterns, calligraphy is an interesting design idea.

Teabags and cucumber slices
A hand-screen-printed (see p. 144) pillowcase by Jon Lys Turner, who discovered a wide range of subtle shades in these everyday objects.

Pigs and chickens
A dark background enhances the photographic qualities of these silk-screened farmyard images, by Jon Lys Turner.

Insects
Jon Lys Turner has chosen a surprising subject to decorate this hand-painted pillowcase. Delicate patterning and a simple, flecked border demonstrate an effective use of one colour.

Egyptian symbols
Inspired by the shapes and colours of Ancient Egypt, Carolyn Quartermaine has used a pigment-based professional fabric paint to achieve purity of colour. The fabrics are Irish linen and fine cotton.

Textured details
A chalky, painted effect, suitable for the subject, has been achieved by using very opaque fabric paint and white pigment.

sponged (see page 127) effect on top of a complementary dye-could complete a dazzling set of bed-linen. If you are painting on to a dyed background, you should make sure that the colours will show up when printed: a yellow fabric paint used straight from the pot, for example, will not show up on a red or blue background unless the fabric paint is mixed with white first. As a general rule, always use an opaque or a pearlized fabric paint when painting on strongly coloured backgrounds.

When decorating bed-linen, consider teaming it with matching accessories such as hangers, cushions and fabric-covered boxes to give your bedroom a pretty co-ordinated look.

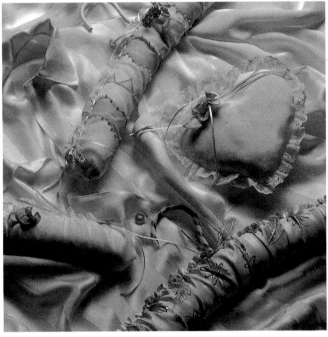

Silk hangers and heart
Gill Dickinson hand painted pure silk fabric before making it up into these coat hangers and this scented heart. She used ribbons, beads and embroidery to highlight the soft colours and delicate motifs. Fabric paints or silk paints can be diluted to produce a water-colour effect (see p. 136).

Heraldic design
Foliage, heraldic shields,
classical lettering and
scrolled shapes all contribute
to the powerful overall
design. The red was printed
after the black, using a
separate screen.

A regal look
Jon Lys Turner, influenced by
heraldic motifs, hand printed
(see page 144) this duvet
cover using limited colours
and strong design. He thus
transformed a plain white
duvet cover and created a
dynamic focal point for the
room.

CONTINUITY OF EFFECT

Simple painting techniques can be used on bed-linen and a range of other soft furnishing items, including accessories like cushions (see page 88) and lampshades (see page 103), in order to give more unity to a room.

A simple two-colour colour scheme could look more exciting if applied using a large, dry household brush – try a bold brush-stroke check across a duvet cover, for example. Don't get carried away by the simplicity of the technique, however. To get the best result it is important to draw chalk guidelines first, and apply the paint in spontaneous brush strokes, while following the chalk marks.

For continuity, a small-scale version of the duvet design could be used on the pillowcases, perhaps in a contrasting white fabric paint. If a totally co-ordinated scheme in a bedroom is the desired effect, then the check could be used as a border on a lampshade, cushions or blinds. This type of geometric design will always look stylish in grey or white with black. If you would prefer a softer colour scheme try duck-egg blue or raspberry pink with grey. Or for a more dramatic, rich look choose navy on deep red or black with purple.

Classical theme
Jon Lys Turner has used a strong colourway in this hand-painted design. The classical themes suggested in the columns and borders are given a contemporary interpretation.

BEDSPREADS

Painted silk bedspreads can look beautiful if painted in soft colours using a simple spray or stencilling technique. To make the bedspread look even more luxurious, quilting and embroidery can be applied afterwards. Since a bedspread is a large area to paint, it is not a good item for the novice to practice on. Even more experienced fabric painters should try and think of ways of painting the bedspread that will be relatively easy yet still give the desired effect. If one or two simple shapes only are

stencilled or printed randomly all over the bedspread (spread out but evenly spaced) this pattern could look effective, especially if embroidered or quilted afterwards.

PAINTING LARGE AREAS

If you do not have enough space to spread out such a large area of fabric (and most of us don't), you can paint the bedspread a section at a time. This is relatively easy if the motifs are well spaced out and regular, but make sure you do not smudge any motifs that have not dried completely. If the occasional smudge does occur, embroidery may save the day and disguise the mistakes. An alternative way of approaching the problem would be to paint the motifs on to the same or similar fabric and then appliqué the painted pieces on to the bedspread.

BORDERS

For some bedspreads a border design painted along the top edge might be more suitable, and the pattern could also be carried through to the edges of the pillowcases. Work out how wide your border should be before you start planning the design.

To make sure the repeated motifs are evenly spread, measure the width of the bedspread and the width of the motif and work out how many you want to paint. Allow for the seam allowance and lightly mark with pencil where each motif should be painted or stencilled. It is a good idea to paint every other motif and then go back and fill in the gaps. This will allow time for the motifs on either side to dry and so reduce the likelihood of smudging.

Painting and stitching
Anne Chiswell stencilled (see page 136) these floral motifs, using soft colours to give ordinary white cotton an expensive look. To increase the luxurious feel, she quilted the fabric, with the stitches following the edges of the motifs.

Stencilled motifs
A simple dashed border, broken by a charming butterfly motif, frames this delicately stencilled cushion. Several shades of one colour are used, created by diluting the fabric paint to make paler shades.

TABLE-LINEN

Nowadays, a tablecloth is not a necessity, but it can, when used in conjunction with beautifully painted napkins and place mats, create a real sense of style. A tablecloth that is very special need only be used occasionally. On a set of napkins, all that may be needed in the way of decoration could be a simple border design or one motif painted in each corner. Try decorating the napkins with the same design and technique, but each one in a different colourway.

But bear in mind that tablecloths do not have to be restricted to the dining room. Small tables in any room can be covered with fabric to co-ordinate with loose covers, or bedside tables can be covered to match a painted quilt or bedspread. Use two different hand-painted fabrics in contrasting designs, perhaps linked by the same tones. Put one over the other and make them different lengths to see how they work together.

Stencilled roses
A plain, circular tablecloth and napkins are enlivened with a repeated stylized rose motif, which was stencilled (see page 132) onto the fabric.

Keep the design simple, and remember that a tablecloth need not have an all-over design. Just a decorative border or geometric pattern may be all that is necessary for your cloth to look wonderfully stylish. In the dining room, where you might be using matching painted napkins and decorative china, you do not want to clutter the table setting. You may want to take the design from your china, to give a co-ordinated look. However simple your design is, it is still a large area of fabric to paint, so work out the design carefully beforehand.

Triangles
This simple white tablecloth and matching napkins have been transformed by the addition of a simple hand-painted border of triangles in primary colours.

If you are thinking of painting a new tablecloth, check the fabric content first. Many new tablecloths and napkins are polyester and cotton, and some paints tend to bleed on this type of fabric. This may be acceptable if your design is a watercolour effect, where the fabric paint has already been diluted, but it could be disastrous if your design is a geometric one with very clean, straight edges. With this type of material, either soften the design or mix the fabric paint to a thicker consistency by using white or a pearlized fabric paint.

CHOOSING AN APPROPRIATE MOTIF

Before painting, make sure that any motifs you are likely to use will be positioned in the most attractive place and that the scale of the decoration is suitable. Work this out on paper first, enlarging or reducing motifs where necessary.

Often, old napkins have an embroidered or lace edge, which could be painted delicately with soft, muted shades using a fine brush. This method can also be applied to the lace edges on tablecloths or used on an old damask tablecloth, where the woven flowers could be highlighted with a subtle combination of pastel colours.

If you are painting a border on to a circular tablecloth, bear in mind that it is harder to match up the design than on a rectangular cloth, so plan it out in advance. Whatever the shape of the cloth, if the design is to be repeated all the way round, first draw up a quarter of the design accurately to scale on a piece of paper and then transfer it to the fabric. If the fabric is quite fine, slip the drawing underneath the cloth and trace the design on to the cloth a quarter at a time. The design can also be painted in four stages if there is not a surface large enough for the whole cloth to be spread out flat.

Roses and checks
This hand-painted fabric effectively combines a rose motif with a stylish chequerboard pattern.

ACCESSORIES

To complete an overall scheme small items, such as picture frames, napkins and bags, may be just the thing to add those important finishing touches. These accessories need to be made from a washable fabric, and cotton is the most suitable to use.

Bought lampshades are normally made of stiffened material of the type used for roller blinds and they are, therefore, ideal surfaces to work on. With light shining through the fabric, many painted designs will look translucent. It is important, though, to bear in mind that colours painted on to the lampshade will affect the colour of the light shining through it. For example, if a

Co-ordinating lampshades
Helen Napper has used two colour moods for this collection of hand-painted lampshades: striking and bold, soft and delicate. They are designed to co-ordinate with the existing room decor.

sponged effect in a cream, pink and peach colourway is used, then the lamp will produce a rosy glow. It is well worth using scraps of coloured paper or fabric held against the lampshade to preview the final effect. Black fabric paint could block out the light altogether, so be careful about using such a solid coverage.

When making your own lampshade, it is important to take into account where the lamp is to be positioned and its intended use – if the light is meant to give just an attractive highlight in a dull corner you can use darker colours than you would if you want to read or work by it.

FLOOR COVERINGS

Since the floor covering sets the tone in any living area, there is a good argument for designing the room from the floor up. Rugs are extremely versatile room accessories. They can change the look of any room, adding colour and pattern, and they are easy to move around and inexpensive to make.

Buying a rug of course is what most of us do, but these can be expensive and finding one to co-ordinate with your existing furnishings can be difficult. Painting your own floor coverings has many advantages: it guarantees you something entirely original, it is economical and you can tailor the colours and design to co-ordinate with the existing patterns in the room.

Obviously when considering design and patterns for a floor, the furniture has to be taken into account. An all-over patterned rug in rich colours may well fit into an interior crammed with decorative antique furniture, and it can also look good in a simply furnished room. Pattern tends to be more acceptable in smaller, contained areas rather than in the form of a huge expanse of highly patterned fitted carpet. Don't fall into the trap of thinking that a hand-painted rug need be multicoloured: a black and white geometric pattern can look just as effective.

Florals and geometrics
This elegant canvas floor rug was hand-painted and stencilled (see p. 132). The soft colours help the contrasting floral border and geometric centre to work well together.

For all-round continuity, consider a pastel-coloured stencilled rug on an otherwise plain floor. The rug could be designed so that it co-ordinates with the rest of the room by incorporating the same stencilled motif used on the walls and fabrics, but perhaps reproduced in a different pattern formation.

Geometrics
This plain sisal mat has been given a new lease of life by the addition of a simple geometric pattern in bright colours. The designer used a cut-out stencil to apply the design (see p. 32). It would work equally well in more muted shades.

Painting an original design on to a piece of heavy canvas, doubled and stitched for strength, will produce a hardwearing covering, and once the fabric paint is fixed, one that is completely washable. Another idea is to paint the canvas rug with a varnish; this gives added protection and a more glazed appearance. Once you have painted your canvas rug and it is completely dry, apply a series of varnish top coats. When applying the varnish, brush it on thinly and quickly using a large brush. Use a polyurethane varnish and thin the first coat with 1 part white spirit to 3 parts varnish. Leave it to dry in a warm room for 6-8 hours and then apply a second coat, also thinned 1:3. A further two or three coats will be necessary to toughen the surface. These coats should be thinned by the addition of 1 part white spirit to 5 parts varnish. As added protection, apply two coats of varnish to the back of the rug as well.

If a textured effect would be more suitable for a particular room, then why not hand-dye a rag rug or paint the smoother types of mattings that are commonly available? For matting, use acrylic or auto paints, not the fabric type.

DESIGN IDEAS

If you are looking for inspiration, a good idea is to use the motifs and patterns of a traditional rug. The designs could easily be interpreted, and simplified if necessary, as flat-painted pattern. The designs of Indian dhurries, for example, with their pastel or bright colours and simple geometric shapes incorporating stripes or borders, easily lend themselves to this type of treatment. As a contrast, a numdah rug is a one-coloured floral design woven in very simplistic floral shapes that could easily be copied. Turkish kelims are also inspiring, and their geometric shapes in rich colours could be translated into flat-paint.

These designs can be found in books and often the actual rugs can be seen on display in department stores. Take along a sketch book and make some notes or quick drawings. If painted well, these rugs could give a *trompe-l'oeil* effect.

Inspiration can also be taken from art. Many modern artists have inspired designers, and some artists have even diversified into fabric design (see page 18). After all, a painted canvas rug could just as easily be a painting if hung on a wall.

Experiment with bold pattern and colour, leaving a section of your design, either on paper or fabric, on the floor so that you can walk round it to see if you really like the effect and if it fits in with the rest of the decor. If pale neutrals are the main colours in a room, then a rug painted in contrasting colours may be an alternative that works well.

A painted rug or floor-cloth can be any size that you can cope with and that is not going to look too overpowering. Whatever its dimensions, always try out your ideas first on paper. Draw to scale and add colour to see if the motifs and colours work well together at that size. While you are working on paper, shapes and colours can be changed, enlarged or reduced until the design looks right. Now is the time to eliminate mistakes and alter colours. Once the fabric has been painted it is too late to find out that your design does not have the effect you wanted.

With rugs intended for a child's room, there is no need to stick to a patterned design. An image of a favourite cartoon character or an animal could be perfect in that setting. Again, draw the image full size on paper first and lay it on the floor to see how it looks. To save time, use coloured shapes and move them around until a satisfactory design is found.

IDEAS INTO REALITY

If painting on canvas, you must first remove the manufacturer's dressing, otherwise the fabric paint will not be permanent. Draw the design on to the fabric, using a pencil, and allow enough space all the way round for the seams. Make sure you have sufficient paint mixed to complete the design. Bear in mind that canvas absorbs quite a lot of paint, and for good, solid coverage more than one coat is likely.

In order to avoid smudging the fresh paint as you stretch over a large piece of canvas, you must have a method of working. Either start from the middle and work out, or begin from one end and work along to the other. Like many rugs with geometric patterns, your rug may have a border. If the border lines need to be straight, use two strips of masking tape and paint between the lines. Spread the paint out as much as possible so that it does not seep underneath the tape. And because paint looks darker when it is wet, allow it to dry before deciding if another coat is required. Remove the tape only when the paint is perfectly dry. Auto spray paints are worth considering as an alternative to fabric paints, since they give good coverage, either as a spray effect or as more solid colour, and they are quick drying and permanent (see page 155).

A textured rug, such as a rag rug, may be more suitable in a bedroom than the hard edges of a painted, traditional type. It could look extremely effective if made from shades of one colour, for example. Mix up fabric paint in various shades and use a combination of techniques such as spraying, spattering and sponging to create variety and interest (see pages 127-31). Paint or dye the individual rags before making up the rug.

The shape and size of the room will determine where your rug will look best. However, on a practical note, try not to place it where it will receive very heavy wear. Although the rug is an inexpensive covering, a lot of time and effort have been put into its design and creation. For these reasons, painted rugs are not suitable for bathrooms and kitchens.

Cowboy mat
Painting a bright design on to plain matting is an ideal way of brightening up a child's room. Auto spray paints (see p 155) are perfect for this type of material.

ONE-OFFS

Many fabric artists work in a variety of areas
within the broad outlines of their craft, and
there now seems to be a growing number of
people producing 'one-off' pieces of work.
Whether for private commission or to adorn
the walls of a public building, these textiles
are totally unique and in this way relate very
closely to traditional paintings. In fact, fabric
designers often exhibit their work in art galleries
or they may work directly with interior
designers and architects, to give individuality
to an otherwise dull office space or to add
colour and interest to people's homes.
Once you have developed your skills as a
fabric decorator, you too can create the kind
of artworks shown in this chapter to decorate
your walls.

WHAT IS A ONE-OFF?

One-off pieces of work come in all guises, from painted screens to banners and wall hangings. Many designers combine painting and printing techniques and use a variety of fabrics in order to create a specific 'look'. Producing your own one-off could well take the place of a bought print or painting. It will probably look more effective and will certainly be much cheaper. But before thinking about what imagery you might use, consider first where this work of art might be placed. The colour scheme is an important consideration. It does not necessarily have to blend in; it could, for example, be the focal point in an otherwise single-coloured room furnished with plain accessories. Think, too, of the space that it is going to fit into.

One-offs, such as banners and wall hangings, suggest large-scale pieces, but the size is up to you. A smaller piece could be much easier to control and therefore could be decorated with a more complicated image, using a combination of techniques.

While experimenting with techniques and fabrics, you might find an image or pattern that you would like to use as a starting

Combining dye and paint
K. Virgils' hand-dyed and painted wall hanging demonstrates the fine art approach to textiles. The fabric has been stitched, folded, painted and layered.

point for your piece of work. Play with pieces of fabric of various shapes and colours and pin them to the space you want to fill to see how they look. The ideas and inspiration that flow from this experimentation are often necessary to fire up the enthusiasm you need when faced with a blank piece of fabric. Look, too, at the work of modern artists. Their use of imagery and colour may give you enough ideas to start you on your way.

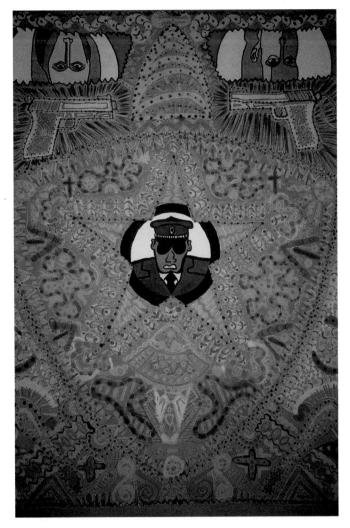

Comic Art
The Bleach Boys use of colours and images give this hand-printed wall hanging a 60s psychedelic feel.

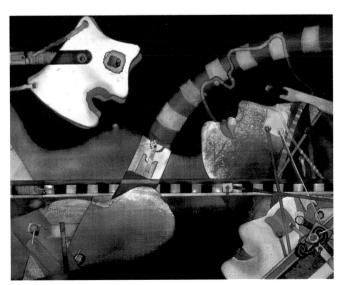

Modern Art
J. Guille's highly original imagery provides another example of the cross-over between textiles and fine art. This piece has been transfer-printed (see page 140) onto a man-made fabric.

MATERIALS AND TECHNIQUES

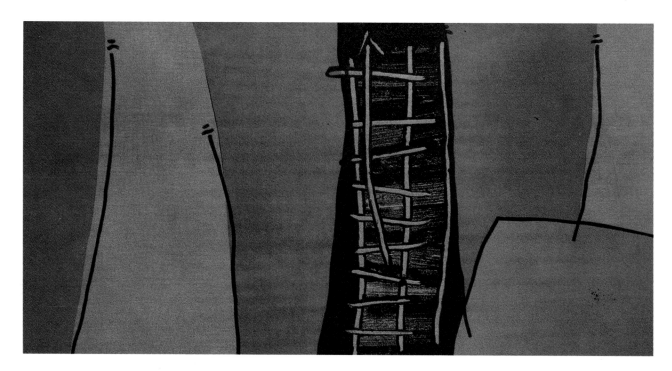

Abstract on wool
Paul Burgess hand painted
this unusual design on to a
wool fabric.

Many fabric artists use types of dye and paint that are not readily available in the shops. This is more economical for them when they are producing a number of large-scale banners or wall hangings. But the commercially available fabric paints are good substitutes and, in most cases, the effects will be exactly the same. A point to bear in mind if you want to design a large wall hanging is the cost. Obviously something of this scale will take up a lot of fabric paint.

A large-scale geometric wall hanging, though, need not necessarily be painted. It could, instead, be dyed. Fabric cut into angular shapes can be dyed different colours, and the pieces stitched together to form a large abstract design. There is no painting or drawing involved in this type of technique, but spend some time arranging the shapes until you think they suit the room. The dyed pieces of fabric could be cut into strips, knotted or woven together. Any type of fabric can be used here, but if you are dyeing the fabric it is best to use material made of natural fibres – even old sheets can be used.

The edges of your wall hangings do not necessarily need to be neatened, since one of the features of this type of project could be the simplistic and slightly haphazard way it is constructed. Nevertheless, this type of wall hanging, with its strong blocks of colour, can be stunning in the right setting.

Silk hangings could be painted using the gutta or wax resist techniques (see page 136). Many traditional wall hangings have

Painted and stitched canvas
K. Virgils stitched together sprayed and dyed canvas shapes to makes this wall hanging.

been made this way. The lines of the gutta or wax are easy to control and the whole process lends itself to experimentation. Still using silk and the same basic technique, a more traditional hanging can be created, such as a single vase of flowers. The design or motif you finally decide on may well have been inspired by an existing fabric or wallpaper.

Stencilling traditional motifs on to silk could also look attractive, especially in a bedroom setting. Stencilled shapes need not always be traditional border bands – all-over patterns can also be used to good effect.

Wall hanging
J. Guille hand painted this fabric, then pleated it to distort the patterning.

UNUSUAL EFFECTS

Pheasants on the cliff path
Nicola Henley hand screen printed this wall hanging. The subtle colouring has been highlighted with hand painting.

Silk wall hangings will often fit into a room better if the surroundings and furnishings are of a similar style. However, some wall hangings make use of dynamic shapes and colours painted on to large pieces of fine wool and silk.

Such a creation in a large high-ceilinged room can be left freehanging, like a banner, and if it is positioned so that the light shines through it, the brilliance of the colours will be enhanced.

A well-lit position is particularly effective with painted silk, producing a magical, translucent effect. Clever artificial lighting can also be used in conjunction with such hangings to produce very exciting results.

For a change of style, painted wall hangings can form the basis of a more co-ordinated scheme, with the same patterning repeated or echoed on the upholstery fabric or floor coverings.

Vibrant hanging
Sian Tucker used professional acid dyes on wool to produce this colourful hand painted wall hanging.

Images for one-offs can be soft and pretty on a small scale or bold and hard-edged on a large scale. Because one-off pieces relate closely to fine art there are no design limitations, just the practical considerations of the technique required to bring them into being.

Try to develop new decorative surfaces by using fabrics, such as felt, that may not usually have a practical use. Although not generally used in the home, felt does not fray and, therefore, edges do not need to be finished. Instead, you could make a feature of the cut edge.

Although wall hangings are unlikely to have to stand a lot of washing, it is best to fix them in order to stop them fading in strong sunlight.

Wall hanging
Jo Pui hand printed and painted this textile as a piece of fabric art.

CHILDREN'S
ROOMS

Put aside your own preferences and prejudices about colour, design and pattern – they do not apply to a child's room. This is their space, and so should reflect their interests, hobbies and ideas. Before even starting to put ideas down on paper, go into the room and take a close look around. Perhaps a theme will immediately jump out at you – a favourite cartoon character, for example, an obvious interest in cars, animals, aeroplanes, boats and so on that can be incorporated into an overall design. Don't forget to consider the little touches and accessories that will help the design work more effectively – bedside lamps, blinds or curtains, duvet covers, pillows and sheets can all become part of an overall look. Wherever possible, try to involve the child in the creation of the designs and patterns, and let him or her, with guidance, have a say in the colours used. Many of the techniques described in this book (see pages 127-152) are perfectly suitable for children to try themselves.

INSPIRATION AND THEMES

Designing and painting fabrics for children's rooms can be fun and very rewarding. Any reservations you have concerning design ideas and colour schemes can all be forgotten. Here your imagination can run riot: colours need not necessarily co-ordinate and designs need not be subtle or fashionably tasteful. Even young children can have strong opinions on how their room should look and they often feel more confident than adults about expressing them. They have no fears over cost, making mistakes or choosing the wrong colours.

Inspiration for designs can be as easy as choosing your child's favourite cartoon character or toy. The objects in the room already play an important part in the atmosphere, so if you are adding to an existing decor, perhaps the hand-decorated fabrics could be a simple extension of this established theme.

Where you are starting from scratch, however, and you are faced with blank walls, then obviously there are a lot more de-cisions to be made. Time, money, size, how much natural light the room receives, as well as the children's ages, are just a few of the important factors that will determine the look of the room.

A room with one dominating theme can be an exciting envi-ronment for children to spend their time in. Choose the theme

Nursery characters
Characters from Beatrix Potter's books feature on this hand-printed fabric by Dragons. You could copy a motif from a nursery paper border to create a similar look, or buy a nursery stencil and paint it onto the fabric and the walls.

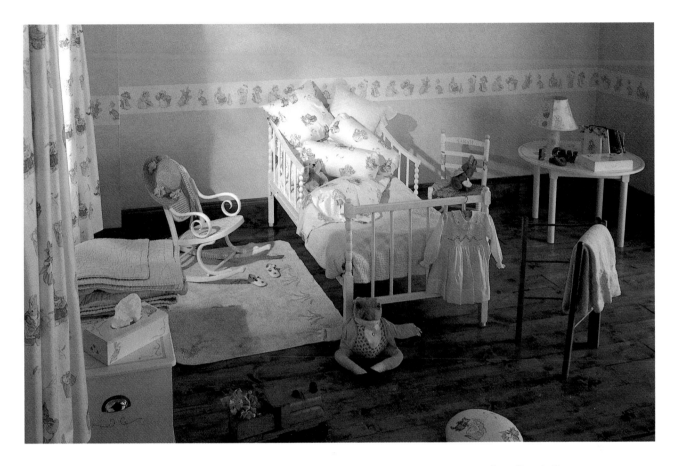

carefully: this month's favourite character or pop star can easily be cast aside in favour of a new one next month. Themes, therefore, need to have a longer life than a fashionable band or a new toy. But the idea need not be too expensive or complicated to produce.

Animal themes are always popular, and these can be used simply in a small, light room. Paw prints, for example, could be made an amusing feature. Copy or trace a paw print from a book, or even use a tracing of the shape of a print from your pet dog or cat. The motif can then be painted onto a blind, across a duvet cover and on to a canvas rug or mat using just a single colour. Or you could cut it from a potato and print it onto the fabric.

It is not necessary to cover a large area with paw prints, in fact the reverse is often more effective – just a row of prints across a duvet to give the impression of the animal having walked across it will have more impact than a random, all-over pattern. Also, it is not practicable for an inexperienced fabric painter to attempt an all-over pattern on a large area such as a duvet cover.

To create a co-ordinated theme, you should first decide on

Beatrix Potter nursery
A favourite nursery theme is used on hand-printed fabric by Dragons for matching curtains, bumpers, footstool and lampshade. The fabric co-ordinates with hand-painted furniture. (If you want to paint furniture to match your fabric, be sure to use non-toxic nursery paint.)

how many surfaces you are going to decorate. Seeing that cartoon characters such as Mickey Mouse are now available on wallpaper and fabric, perhaps painting a large-scale Mickey Mouse on a roller blind would be all that was necessary to create the ideal effect in a child's room – especially since Mickey is one nursery character who does not seem to wane in popularity.

A specially designed mural may need the continuity of motifs added to a blind or fabric to complete the look of the room. It need not be copied exactly, but simple elements taken from the mural could be painted on to the fabric in the form of a border, or simple shapes repeated at intervals.

Hand printed bunnies
Bright hand-screen-printed fabric by Dragons makes attractive bed-linen for a baby's cot. For safety, make sure that any colours used are properly fixed (see page 154).

An economical way of revamping an existing decor is to change the colours of the furnishings, and primary themes are particularly suitable for children. Dull, pastel bed-linen can be transformed by using some brightly coloured dyes. Try dyeing each article a different colour – a bright red duvet cover, for

Children's accessories
Hand-printed Dragons fabric is used to line this toy basket. If you want to tackle more complicated motifs, like these attractive bunnies, a small fabric accessory is an ideal starting point.

Animal motif
This hand-printed fabric by Sally Guy, illustrated in two different colourways, shows that animal images don't have to be realistic to be successful. Here, a naive style gives great impact.

example, with blue sheets and yellow pillowcases. Small items such as pillowcases can be hand dyed, but sheets and duvet covers should be dyed separately in a washing machine (see page 150). It is not worth trying to dye large items by hand since results are often patchy. By using a washing machine you get perfect colour distribution and depth of colour with a lot less effort than is required for hand dyeing.

Before dyeing, you should think carefully about the colour changes. If the item is already coloured, you cannot dye it a particular shade unless you first strip the existing colour from the fabric (see page 150).

ACCESSORIES TO PAINT

Small items and accessories can be painted to add interest to an already exciting children's room. This may be preferable for a beginner, who might think that painting a duvet cover is too much to contemplate.

As a first step, why not consider a drawstring canvas bag as an ideal start to fabric decoration? The fabric could be painted before the bag is made or it is just as easy to paint it after it has been made up. The design can be as simple or as complicated as you want it to be. A multicoloured spattered bag will look fun hanging behind the door; and toy bags with the contents or children's names stencilled on to the fronts are original as well as making a personal statement.

Scottie dog toy bag
Gill Dickinson has used an appealing scottie dog motif and geometrics to makes this delightful toy bag. The design is hand painted, and a stippled effect has been used to produce a sense of texture. The fabric bows were sewn on afterwards.

Scottie lampshade
Using the same basic design as for the bag, this lampshade is perfect for a child's bedroom. The straight lines were painted with the help of masking tape and the scotties were applied with a stencil. Light shining through the shade does not dilute the vivid primaries.

INVOLVING THE CHILD

Dyed bed linen (see page 120) could be combined with a painted effect, such as spattering (see page 130) or sponging (see page 127). And these techniques could easily benefit from the enthusiastic help of children. Spattering a duvet cover can be fun for any one to do. Before you start, take care to prevent any messy accidents by protecting clothing and any vulnerable surfaces that are not to be covered in paint. When spattering, paint will fly quite a way, so protect all the surrounding area. Better still, carry out these messy techniques outside where everyone can join in without worry.

Ready cut stencils using images suitable for children are now widely available, and it is worth looking at these before attempting your own. A simple stencil of letters and numbers can be used to great effect by painting them on to fabric, using felt tip fabric pens. Either use the motifs in a random arrangement or place names or words along borders or in stripes. This very easy technique can give a plain room its own individual appeal.

Children can also use their own drawings and paintings as fabric decoration. The starting point could be something they have produced at school or something specially designed for the room. The drawings can easily be enlarged for a blind or painted directly on to a lampshade in exactly the same way as painting on to paper. Make sure, however, that the fabric is compatible with the fabric paint you want to use.

For more information on techniques that are suitable for children to attempt see page 151.

Colour-in duvet
This duvet cover by Maison has a printed outline for the child to colour-in with fabric crayons (see pages 32 and 154). To create this type of cover yourself, draw on the outline (traced from a book or magazine if necessary) with a black, fabric felt pen, then hand the cover over to the child with a pack of fabric crayons. (Make sure you supervise the fixing stage though!)

TECHNIQUES

This chapter outlines the basic steps you must follow to carry out the popular fabric decoration techniques successfully. One of the most satisfying aspects of fabric painting and printing is that, even as a complete novice, you can achieve a pleasing result – if, of course, you select the appropriate technique. As is the case with many other fields of endeavour, with fabric decoration you will need a period of trial and error while you learn the strengths and weaknesses of the elements you are using – the fabric, paints and any equipment – and how they work best together to produce the result you want. As an aid to your confidence, in the beginning start with small pieces of fabric or at least large pieces of inexpensive material. This way you will not worry too much if you make a few mistakes. As you become more used to the basic techniques, you will find that the technically more advanced procedures are less daunting.

BEFORE YOU START

Fabric painting techniques such as sponging and spattering are easy to achieve as they require virtually no drawing skills. However, a reasonable eye for colour and a clear idea of the type of effect you would like to see will help. All of the painted effects can be combined in one design if desired and on any type of fabric. The effect can be soft and pretty if you use a silky or sheer fabric with a pastel colour scheme, or bold and brilliant if you use a heavy canvas and primary, vibrant or dark, dramatic colours.

Before you start any technique, it is important to try out different colour combinations on scraps of fabric until you find ones you particularly like and which will work with other colour scheme ideas. The designs need not be planned too precisely since these techniques are quite spontaneous, and often the best results happen by accident.

GETTING THE RIGHT RESULTS

If you want to make a success of your fabric decoration just follow a few basic points that are common to all of the following techniques and you cannot go far wrong.

1 Have the appropriate equipment to hand: rags, sponges, brushes, water jars, etc.

2 Cover all vulnerable surfaces, and if the paint does splash on a surface, remove it quickly before it dries.

3 Using old saucers and jars, mix enough paint to make sure that you complete the design.

4 Stretch the fabric out and secure it on a slightly padded, but flat, surface with masking tape. A low-tack masking tape will keep the fabric taut and it will not mark the surface when removed.

5 Ideally, you should have enough space to stretch the fabric out completely. However, if this is not possible the fabric can be painted in sections by laying it out on a table partly folded and moving it around, making sure each section is dry before you start the next, until the design has been completed.

6 Make sure that there are no gaps in the design. For example, take care to overlap the sponging or spattering so that there are no unintentional blank areas.

7 Try to leave the fabric to dry before moving it to paint another section. This will eliminate the possibility of smudging.

8 When your painted or printed decoration is dry, you must fix the fabric (see page 155).

Note: Advice for the beginner is also given in the Basics chapter, pages 24-37.

SPONGING

Natural sea sponges are traditionally used for this technique, but they are expensive. As an alternative, you can use ordinary household sponges, screwed-up rags or, in fact, any material that might give an interesting texture when dabbed on to the fabric (for example, a piece of old lace painted and pressed on to the surface can give a fascinating mesh print). One or all of these can be used in the same design.

Apply the paints from saucers or old plates. Jars are not suitable since you need to press the sponge or rag into the paint. You can, though, mix the colour in jars and pour it out as you need it. Any paint left over can be stored for quite some time. Each colour needs a separate plate or saucer. You should have more than one piece of sponge or rag, changing over when the first one becomes saturated. Use both sides of the sponge as well as the ends to vary the effect.

Dip the sponge into the palest colour first, lightly so as not to overload it with paint. Shake off any excess and press the sponge down on to a scrap of fabric or paper. The first print is often too thick and the texture does not show through. Continue pressing the sponge down randomly all over the fabric, keeping the prints quite evenly spaced. Keep on sponging until you need to reload with paint again. Change the colour and the sponge when necessary. The same sponge can be used for different colours as long as you wash it thoroughly in water first. The fabric paint will stain the sponge, but if you allow it to dry before re-using it, this will not matter.

You do not have to wait for the first layer of sponge paint to dry, before staring the next. Overlap the colours to create different hues and continue until you are satisfied with the colour combinations and the coverage. You may, of course, want some background fabric colour to show through – these design decisions are entirely personal.

Equipment
Masking tape
Saucers/plates/screw-top jars
Paints
Sponges/rags
Water jar
Absorbent paper
Old blanket
Clean cloth for fixing

1

2

1. Mix colours, putting a small amount in a saucer. Dip in the sponge, pressing the first print onto spare paper to get rid of excess paint. Dab onto fabric, leaving small gaps.

2. Wash sponge and leave to dry – a wet sponge won't show texture. Repeat Step One with the second colour, filling gaps and overlapping the first colour.

3. Two-colour sponging will create a third colour where overlapping occurs.

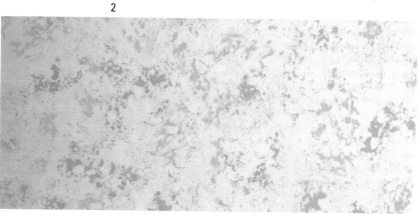

3

SPRAYING

A fine spray of paint, for a multicoloured or single-coloured effect, can be achieved using a variety of methods. The quickest and most efficient way is to use an airbrush. This is an expensive piece of equipment, however, and unless you are going to spray a lot of fabric, it is not worthwhile investing in one. A diffuser gives the same effect and can be bought very cheaply, but obviously it is more mechanical and slower to use.

To use a spray diffuser you need to blow through a mouthpiece attached to one end of a tube while the other end is immersed in diluted fabric paint. Tilt the spray hole towards the fabric while blowing and a fine spray will be emitted. Repeat this technique over the fabric, wash out the diffuser with water, change the colour and repeat.

The fabric paint has to be diluted to a very watery consistency or it will block the diffuser. But despite this, the spray is so fine that colour bleeding is not a problem. A garden spray can also be used but it will not produce such a fine, delicate result.

An old toothbrush is another piece of equipment that can be used for this technique, and it is not necessary to dilute the fabric paint. Dip the toothbrush into the paint and shake off any excess so that you do not deposit blobs of colour on the fabric. Hold the brush over the fabric and rub your finger along the bristles until a spray of paint lands on the fabric. Wash out the toothbrush, wipe it until it is almost dry and repeat the process using the other colours.

By masking off areas or using stencils, sprayed shapes can be created, as well as an all-over spray. Don't remove tape or stencil until the paint is dry.

Auto spray paints can be used on fabrics, but only on those that are not to be washed, such as roller blinds. Frequently washed or fine fabrics are not suitable. Auto spray paints are not water-soluble, so care is necessary when using them. They dry quickly and once sprayed on to any surface they are permanent. This type of paint also has a tendency to stiffen fabrics.

Equipment

Masking tape
Saucers/plates/screw-top jars
Paints
Water jar
Old toothbrush or spray diffuser
Old blanket
Clean cloth for fixing

1. If you are using a diffuser, dilute the fabric paint so that it flows freely down it. If you are using a toothbrush, pour a small amount of paint on to a saucer and dip the bristles lightly into it. Wash diffuser and brush before changing colours.

1

2. Fill a container half full of diluted fabric paint. Immerse the end of the diffuser in it and hold on to the mouth-piece. Position the container about 15 cm (6 in) above the fabric and tilt it towards it.

3. Blow through the mouthpiece so that the spray lands on the fabric. For a finer spray move further away from the fabric. If the diffuser becomes blocked, run water through it a few times. To get an even coverage move across the fabric while you spray.

2

3

4

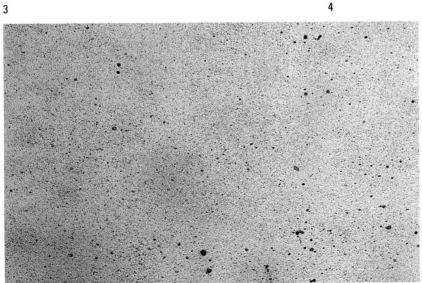

4. To use the toothbrush, hold it above the fabric and rub your finger along the bristles so that a fine spray is created. Don't put too much paint on the brush or you will produce blobs. Repeat the toothbrush technique over the whole fabric.

5. If you want to create a multi-coloured sprayed effect, use both toothbrush and diffuser. Use the diffuser for a fine background spray and the toothbrush for a more definite spray on top. Spray each colour separately, starting with the lightest and building gradually. You will find that colours overlap to produce many more tones and shades.

5

SPATTERING

Splashing or spattering fabric can be fun and effective, and it looks best if bright colours are used. This means that colours can be used unmixed straight from the pot. Although it is the easiest technique, it is probably also the messiest, particularly if you have a large piece of fabric to cover. Be careful to protect carpets, walls and other surfaces before starting. If you have a garden, and the weather is fine, it might be a good idea to work outdoors.

For this technique, all you need do is dip the end of a brush or stick into the paint and flick it on to the fabric. Repeat this until you have the coverage you want and then wipe the stick and change colours. Change direction and flick from different distances and angles just to vary and overlap the spatters. This method is most effective when the majority of the fabric is spattered. Bear in mind that the fabric will look more covered with paint when flat than it will when hanging down.

Spattering does take some time to dry, since some of the blobs of paint will be quite thick. Carefully blot any very dense blobs with paper and dry the fabric with a hairdryer held about 15-30 cm (6-12 in) away from the surface of the fabric. Alternatively, leave the fabric to dry in the garden. If you hang the fabric on a line some of the blobs of paint may run, but since this effect is so informal it should not matter.

Equipment
Masking tape
Saucers/plates/screw-top jars
Selection of brushes
Absorbent paper
Water jar
Hairdryer
Old blanket
Clean cloth for fixing

1. Secure the fabric with masking tape and protect vulnerable surfaces from paint splashes. Mix the colours or use direct from the pots.

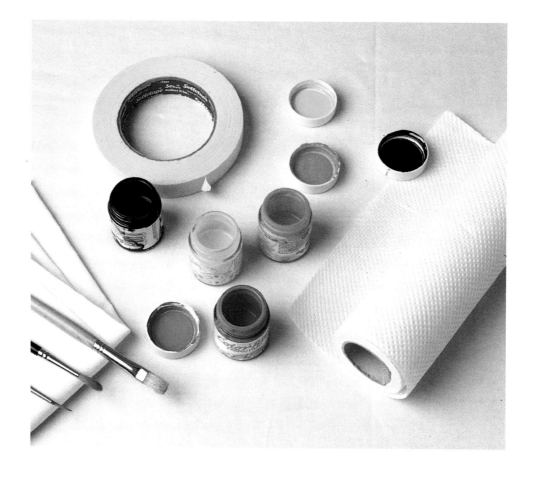

2

3

4

2. Using the end of a brush or a stick, dip into the pot and flick paint all over the fabric using a brisk wrist action. When the paint runs out re-apply. Use several colours, wiping the end of the brush or stick before changing colour.

3. Change your direction of flicking so that spatters are in different directions and overlap. And vary your distance from the fabric so that spatters differ in shape and size. If some of the blobs are too thick with paint, blot them with a piece of rag or paper. This also speeds up the drying process. (Use a hairdryer to speed up drying further.)

4. Keep on adding colours, but leave black until last so that it does not dominate. This type of patterning is more successful when very little background colour shows through.

5. Leave the fabric until perfectly dry before ironing to make permanent.

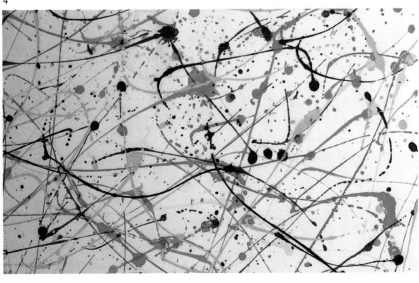

5

STENCILLING

When stencilling, the simplest patterns are often the most successful. Sketch out some design ideas for cutting your own stencils on paper first, making sure that the design motifs are not too close together. If the gaps, or 'bridges', are too narrow, the cut stencil could easily tear. Bridges at frequent intervals help to strengthen the stencil as well as forming an integral part of the pattern.

Next, draw the designs to actual size, and use low-tack masking tape (which will not mark the fabric) to attach the sketch to the surface you intend to stencil on. This will give you an idea of scale and you will also be able to see if the design is suitable.

Colour is obviously of great importance, and even the simplest of patterns can be enhanced by the right combination of shades. If you already have a background colour, try out different colour combinations before making a final decision. This can be made easier by painting an area of each colour roughly the size of your stencil and attaching these to the surface to be stencilled. This will give you an accurate idea of how the colours work together. It is worth spending time at this stage trying variations and experimenting before starting on the actual fabric.

Home-made and ready-cut stencils

Useful sources of inspiration for patterns are books, magazines and fabric swatches. Design motifs can easily be traced off and squared paper can help you to enlarge or reduce the size of a motif. However, if you do not want to create your own stencils you may find a suitable design from the many ready-cut stencils available. These can be expensive, but they are very accurately cut out and they are re-usable. Stencils range from elaborate motifs to simple,

traditional numbers and letters available in book form or as individual designs.

Ready-cut stencils still involve a lot of creativity, since choice of colour and positioning of the motifs are vital to a successful result. Stencils in book form are clearly printed on card, ready to cut out. But before doing this, prepare the card by rubbing linseed oil and turpentine into it to make it more pliable.

Stencils can be cut from any type of card, but the most suitable materials to use are oiled stencil card and acetate or mylar. Oiled stencil card is sold in sheets and it is quite hard wearing. The advantage of using this special card is that it does not soak up the paint but, being opaque, the design has to be transferred on to the card before cutting. Oiled stencil card is cheaper than acetate, it is good for small intricate designs and it is less likely to split.

Acetate or mylar is sold in sheets or pads and, although more expensive, it has the advantage of being transparent. Designs, therefore, can be transferred directly on to it. This is particularly useful if you are cutting two or three stencils for different colour areas, since it is easier to line the designs up with one another. Also, paint just wipes off this material, making it ideal for use at a later date.

Cutting the stencil

First, transfer your design to the stencil card or acetate. Make sure the design is placed centrally, leaving at least 2.5 cm (1 in) all the way round. If you are using card, the easiest way to transfer the design is to put carbon paper between the design and the stencil card. Then, using a knitting needle, press down lightly with the tip of the needle around the outline of the design. The design

should now be transferred to the card.

If you are using acetate, just place it over the top of the design and draw the shape onto it with a fine ballpoint pen. Designs to be stencilled in more than one colour need a separate stencil cut for each colour. To cut the stencil card or acetate, attach it to a flat, smooth surface (preferably glass) with masking tape. Cutting the stencil on glass gives a very clean cutting edge. Wooden cutting boards can be used, but sometimes the knife sticks in the wood causing a jagged edge on the stencil. If using a glass cutting surface, always cover the edges with tape for safety. Use a sharp knife, or scalpel, for intricate designs, and start by cutting the smaller shapes first. Hold the knife firmly and cut towards you. Try to keep the cutting action continuous so that the cut stencil edges are smooth. If you do end up with any jagged edges on the stencil card, smooth them off with fine sandpaper afterwards.

Stencil registration

If you are using more than one colour, fitting the stencils together so that each part of the design is in the right place can sometimes be tricky. Using acetate makes this task easier because it is transparent. With a ballpoint pen, just mark on each sheet of acetate key areas of the design, and align these marks when painting the stencil.

If you are using stencil card, registration can be a little more difficult. Transfer each colour on to a separate stencil and then cut out and line up the stencils so that they fit together. Trim the stencils to exactly the same size and then punch registration notches through all the pieces of card simultaneously. By matching up the notches, the design should fit together perfectly each time.

How to stencil

It is always a good idea to practise a few times on scraps before stencilling on purchased fabric. Always prepare the surface beforehand (see page 126) and if you are stencilling on to new fabric remove any finish it might have.

Mix all the paints and have them conveniently to hand. Make sure the paint is the right consistency – not too thin or it will run. Attach the stencil to the surface with tape or pins. Gently dip the tip of the brush into the paint and dab the brush up and down (this action is called pouncing) on a clean sheet of paper. This distributes the paint evenly and removes any excess – if you have too much paint on the brush it will seep under the stencil.

Holding the stencil brush firmly, pounce the paint through the cuts in the stencil. Use a rocking motion and pounce from the edges to the middle of the stencil until all the gaps are painted. Leave the painted fabric to dry before removing the stencil. A traditional stencil brush gives the best results, but for large areas an ordinary decorator's brush could be used. If you want a more textured finish try using a marine sponge or a crumpled piece of cloth to apply the paint. For more detailed work, a small artist's brush would be useful to touch in any awkward areas.

If you are painting a multicoloured stencil, complete everything in one colour first, allow it to dry, and then start the next colour. If you are working across the fabric, stencil alternate motifs in one direction and then work back in the other to avoid smudging the still wet paint with your hand.

Equipment
Stencil brush
Stencil card or acetate
Sharp craft knife or scalpel
Saucers or palettes
Masking tape
Clean water
Clean rags
Sheet of glass or cutting board
Ruler
Pencils

1. Prepare the materials, mix paints, stretch out the fabric and lay the ready cut-out stencil in position over the top. Pour out the mixed fabric paint into a saucer and have a clean rag or paper at hand. Dip the stencil brush into the paint and, with a dabbing movement (called pouncing), get rid of excess paint onto the scrap of cloth or paper. When the brush is almost dry, 'pounce' onto the stencil until all areas are covered.

1

2. Leaving the stencil in place, check that all the areas of the pattern have been evenly painted. Make sure that the paint is thoroughly dry before removing the stencil. If the paint is wet removing the stencil could easily damage it.

3. Stencils can be re-used, to repeat a motif, and reversed. Let the stencil dry before using it again, so as not to mark the fabric or spoil the colour.

2

3

4

4. Hold the stencil in place with one hand so that it is quite secure. Any movement might spoil the image and smudge the stencilled motif. If the cut stencil is of a delicate motif, with narrow spaces between the 'bridges', make sure that the loaded brush is very dry so the paint does not seep underneath the stencil and spoil the effect.

5. Remove all stencils when the design is perfectly dry. Clean and store the stencils and brush for future use. If any areas need touching up, use a small brush and paint in. Fix (make permanent) the design by covering the fabric with a clean cloth and ironing for a few minutes with an iron set to medium hot.

5

SILK PAINTING

Silk paints appear transparent but, when painted on to silk, they become quite brilliant and translucent. Some professional silk paints have to be steam-fixed, but most commercially bought ones are simpler to use. They need either ironing or completely immersing in a fixative solution for about five minutes. Once this has been done, the paint is permanent and the fabric is washable.

All silk paints are intermixable, and can be diluted to form paler shades. If you are covering a large area of silk in a single colour, add a few drops of diffusing agent (available in most shops and department stores where silk paints are sold) to the paint. This will help to give an even coverage without any hard brushstroke lines.

Silk paints can be used to create a number of effects. Painting on to a wet surface, for example, softens and merges colours (see page 29); while using paints with a resist, such as wax or gutta, will create a more controlled design. Again, before tackling a project, you should experiment with different densities of paint, from full strength to very diluted, and try different types and sizes of brush on scraps of silk.

Once you are familiar with the silk paint, you will be able to determine the type of design you would like to create. Obviously, a hard-edged geometric pattern is not suitable, since these paints flow on to the fabric. Perhaps, initially, you should treat your design like a painting. An ideal shape of fabric to start on is a square of silk for a cushion or scarf. Floral motifs are good subjects for beginners. You could trace shapes from books or magazines if you don't have enough confidence in your drawing skills.

Applying gutta

Gutta is sold in bottles and is a gum-like solution that acts as a resist (just like wax in batik), and comes in black, clear, gold and silver. When dry, it acts like a barrier, preventing colours merging into each other on the silk.

To use the gutta you need a nib or, for a fine outline, a small plastic applicator with the nozzle pierced with a pin. When applying the gutta to the fabric, turn the applicator upside down at intervals to stop any air bubbles forming. After use, clean the applicator with white spirit. A few drops of special solvent can be added if the gutta becomes too thick. Don't add too much, though, or the gutta may bleed and not be sufficiently strong enough to act as an effective barrier.

The sequence of events

Before you start to paint, you must wash out any manufacturer's dressing from the fabric. Then stretch the silk on to a flat surface or a wooden frame using drawing pins or masking tape to hold the fabric taut. If you are following a drawing or design, slip this underneath the frame, making sure you can see through the silk to the drawing beneath. Using your drawing as a guide, apply the gutta, following all the outlines, and make sure it penetrates to the back of the silk. When the gutta is dry (after about an hour), you can start to paint your design.

Mix all your colours before you start to paint, making sure that you mix enough of the background colour. Dip a soft brush into the silk paint and apply colour to the centre of the section you are working on. Paint quickly, pushing the silk paint as far as it will go into that section before reloading the brush. It is best to use a little at a time, especially if you are working on very fine silk. If necessary, dilute the silk paint to give a colourwash effect. Add more water or silk paint as you go along to create different tones and shades if you need them. Wash the brushes and squeeze out any excess water before changing colours, so that you keep the colours pure. If the paint does not dry smoothly, add a few drops of a compatible solvent to prevent hard lines appearing and give a flatter surface. When the design is completed and perfectly dry, soak the silk in a compatible fixative solution for five minutes.

The fabric paint is now permanent and washable. Once the fabric has been fixed you can remove the gutta by ironing the fabric between two sheets of clean paper. An outline of the background fabric colour will be left if you have used clear gutta. If, however, you have used black, gold or silver gutta, then an outline in these colours will remain as part of your design.

Equipment

Layout paper
Pencil
Paints or crayons
Felt-tip pen
Silk paints
Diffusing agent
Wooden frame
Masking tape or drawing pins
Water jar
Selection of brushes
Fixative (if necessary)
Paper
Gutta
Gutta applicator
Specialist solvent (for gutta)

1

2

3

4

5

1. Sketch your rough ideas before you embark on the finished design. Then, draw it to scale, using a pencil.

2. Colour in the design, using paints or crayons, before you paint the silk, so that you have a rough idea of the finished result. Choose soft pastels and try to achieve water-colour quality by diluting the paints.

3. Once you have finalized the colours, trace the design on to a separate piece of layout paper using felt-tip pen. This outline will act as a guide when you come to carefully paint the gutta resist on to the silk.

4. Lay the tracing on a flat surface and secure with masking tape. Then lay a piece of crease-free silk over the top and also secure with masking tape. Fill the applicator with gutta. Following the outline, carefully paint the gutta resist on to the silk.

5. When the gutta outline is dry, mix all your colours. Use a small brush to paint the background colours. Once dry, paint the individual flowers. Wash the brush carefully before changing colours.

6. Fix the design by immersing in fixative for five minutes. Wash and dry the fabric. The gutta will wash out and you will see an outline formed by the ground colour.

6

BLOCK PRINTING

Block printing can be either extremely simple or extremely complicated. The most basic form of block printing is one that most of us tried as children – cut a potato, carrot or pear in half, leave it to dry out for half an hour, paint the cut surface and then press it down on to a piece of paper or fabric. This is by far the cheapest and easiest way of repeating a motif over a piece of fabric. If something as simple as a spotted design is required, then the cross-section of a carrot is perfect. But anything with a raised or textured surface can be used employing exactly the same basic technique. Just repaint the cut surface when the print starts to lose its colour and strength.

By changing the colours and repeating the block print in different directions, or by overlapping the motifs, more interesting patterns begin to emerge. It may be helpful to carry out some trial prints on paper first. Cut these out and move them around on the fabric until you like the arrangement. A random repeating design using more than one 'found' object to print with can look effective, but make sure enough space is left in between the first printed shapes to print in another, otherwise the design could look unbalanced. If you are printing with a cardboard shape, such as the open end of a matchbox, paint the narrow rectangular shape, press it down on to the fabric, and then wipe the surface with a dry cloth before changing colours. You will need to have a few matchboxes to hand, since the card will become soggy fairly quickly and so will need replacing.

An easy, and more versatile, way of block printing is to have a selection of wooden blocks with raised shapes glued down to them. Rope or string is particularly good to use, since it can be coiled and manipulated into a great variety of shapes. Glue the rope or string to the block, paint the raised surface and then press it on to the fabric. Not only will the shape be printed but the texture of the rope or string itself will provide additional interest. An infinite number of shapes can be printed in this way, providing a much more sophisticated design.

It is easy to use shapes glued to blocks for random, all-over, repeating designs, but if you wish to create a border or a more regimented repeat, you will need to work this out before starting to print. Measure your fabric width and the motif and calculate how many can be printed across the fabric. By making registration marks on the fabric, using either tailor's chalk or a light pencil, you should be able to gauge where to print the next shape. Fine cotton thread stretched across the fabric in a grid can also be used as a guide, but you need to ensure that the block print shape won't overlap the thread, otherwise a line will appear across your finished print.

I don't want to dwell on the types of repeats, since trying to repeat motifs in obvious patterns can often lead to the sort of design you could have bought ready-printed. Much better is to experiment by playing around with shapes and colours and irregular forms of repeat. Do this and the results will be a lot more interesting.

Equipment

Brushes
Glue
Small wooden blocks
Water jars
Rope or string
'Found' objects
Clean rags/brushes

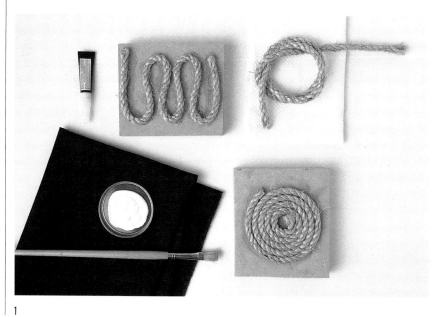

1. Use wooden blocks with one flat surface. Attach the rope with strong glue in your chosen arrangement.

1

2

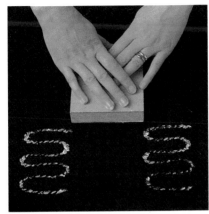

3

4

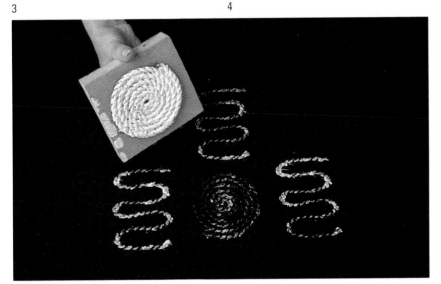

5

2. Stretch out the fabric and secure it with masking tape. Work out your design, deciding where each motif is to be repeated. Either measure the distances between the motifs and lay contrasting threads in a grid to act as a guideline, or judge by eye. Using a white, opaque fabric paint, thick in consistency, paint the rope surface. Be careful not to apply too much, and avoid getting paint on the block itself.

3. Turn the block over and press the rope into the fabric. Press evenly, then lift carefully. If necessary reapply paint to make the next print. Usually the rope can be printed twice before this is necessary. The second print may be slightly more faded, but the texture of the rope will still show.

4. Take your second block and print in alternate spaces. This allows motifs to dry without getting smudged. Avoid putting paint in between the coils.

5. You may find that the coil block does not print as well as the first design. If necessary, reapply the paint and print again.

6. Work the whole pattern and leave it to dry before fixing by ironing. You can use this design to cover a large area, or you could use it as a border. You will find that each print is different from the last, but this is part of the charm of this technique.

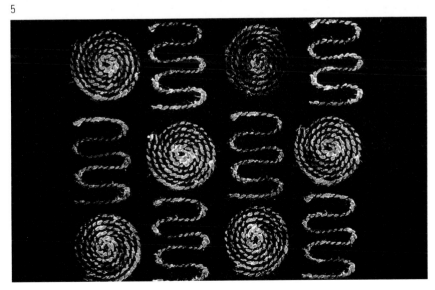

6

TRANSFER PRINTING

This method of decorating fabrics looks best when colours and textures are present in abundance. Where flat, simple designs or two-coloured effects are called for, screen printing (see page 144) or stencilling (see page 132) would be more suitable.

Transfer printing involves using an iron to transfer a pattern from paper on to fabric. Many of the techniques used to colour paper are, therefore, suitable for transfer printing. By using special transfer inks and crayons, in the same way as you would ordinary inks and crayons, an almost infinite number of design and colour ideas can be created.

Suitable fabrics

Although the design permutations are vast, the technique is limited to man-made fabrics. If transfer inks or crayons are used on natural fabrics, colours will be very pale. With mixed fabrics you get a pastel effect which is only suitable on something like polyester-cotton sheets. To see how colours will react to your fabric, test the inks and crayons first on pieces of scrap material.

Making a transfer print

Transfer crayons come in small packets and look very much like a conventional packet of crayons. The transfer inks come in small bottles, usually in sets of eight. For more ambitious projects, large size bottles are also available.

Initially, draw your designs on paper and then paint them using the special inks and crayons. Transfer inks and crayons look particularly dark and dull before they are printed. This can be misleading because once transferred they appear vivid, some almost fluorescent. This is why it is so important to test each colour before using it. When the colour is dry, place the paper, pattern side down, on a piece of polyester or some other suitable fabric. To transfer the design, iron the paper for a few minutes using a medium-hot iron. Use even pressure when ironing, otherwise the colour distribution will be patchy. Because you are ironing paper, you must be careful to keep the iron moving all the time. This is perfectly safe as long as the iron's setting is not too hot.

How the design is ironed on to the fabric has an important effect on the finished result. So to start with, limit the size of the design. When ironing a large area of paper on to fabric, it can easily move and form a double image. Also, with a large design it is difficult to get even coverage and results are nearly always inconsistent. If you are transfer printing a large piece of fabric, try and build up the design by ironing in motifs and textures in sections from smaller pieces of paper.

This is the only technique where all the colours can be printed at once, even inks and crayons can be used together on the same design. For really consistent transfer of colour, a special press can be used instead of an iron. However, this is an expensive piece of equipment, and not really worth the cost unless you intend to produce transfer prints on a commercial basis.

Transfer printing suggestions

Here are some suggestions that you can use, either separately or together, in order to help you to get the 'feel' of the inks and crayons. Start with six pieces of A4 layout paper, a selection of transfer inks and a packet of crayons. Paint and crayon a different pattern or effect on each piece of paper, using as many colours as you like. Combine the crayons and inks wherever possible. Try wetting a piece of paper before applying the transfer inks so that the colours blend and merge.

For another effect, use the crayons and take rubbings from a variety of raised or textured surfaces. In this way you will build up a selection of multicoloured effects. Leave the painted layout paper to dry before transfer printing.

Stretch out a piece of polyester or some other man-made fabric, approximately 60 cm (24 in) square. Have an iron ready, set to medium, and use some bigger pieces of paper to shield the fabric from direct contact with the iron. Obviously, a man-made fabric is more likely to burn than a cotton one, but since the pattern is transferred by heat, the iron does have to be fairly hot. Test different temperatures on scraps of fabric until you can successfully transfer the design without the cloth or paper burning or distorting.

Starting with any of the painted layout papers, cut or tear shapes out and place them face down on the fabric. If they are close together, cover them with another piece of plain paper to shield the fabric and apply heat for about one minute. Gently lift one corner of a pattern piece, just to check that the colour density is strong enough. Tear and cut out other shapes, overlapping them this time, to see how the patterns and colours change.

Try out different ideas until a particular effect appeals to you, and then use it as a theme or an individual element in a separate design or project.

With such random patterns it is hard to make mistakes, but later, when creating a more controlled design, any mistakes can be cut out from the paper before being ironed down. If you are planning to use any kind of lettering or writing, bear in mind that everything prints in reverse, like a mirror image. With practice, more adventurous designs can be attempted, and any gaps appearing in the design can be filled by ironing on individual motifs.

If you want to keep part of the background colour, place plain pieces of paper between the fabric and the design. The paper will act as a barrier preventing any colour transferring. These spaces can be either left plain or other motifs can be worked into them. Remember, each time a pattern or motif is ironed down the colour loses some of its strength, so each print from the same piece of paper will become paler and paler. The fabric does not need fixing and is fully washable.

As long as the ironing stage is always carefully supervised, transfer printing is an ideal technique for children to experiment with.

Equipment

Transfer paints/crayons
Water jar
Selection of brushes
Thin paper (layout type)
Iron
Scissors
Pencils

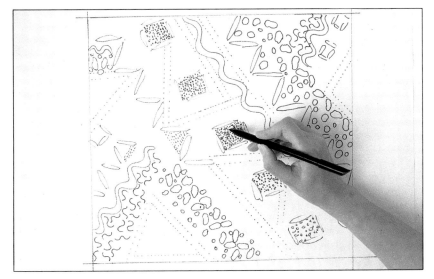

1. Make some preliminary sketches and then plan out your design to scale, using a pencil. Thin paper, such as layout paper, is best, so that the design can transfer to the fabric successfully. Use the colours direct from the transfer paint pots (shaken), or mix colours by diluting with water, to get paler shades.

1

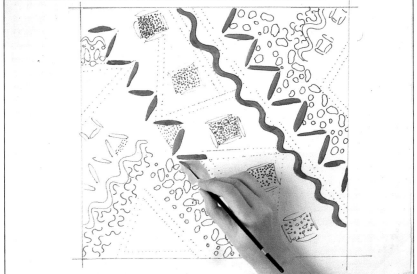

2. Paint the design using the transfer paints. Wash the brush in between colours. Paint the flat areas of colour, but use a brushstroke effect (see page 24).

2

3. Use a toothbrush to add textured spots and dashes. Dip the brush lightly into the paint. With dabbing movements, gently press the bristles on to the design. Repeat until you need to reapply paint. Wash the brush and shake off excess moisture before changing to another colour.

4. Complete the design. You can remove unwanted splashes of colour or mistakes by cutting them out of the paper before transferring to the fabric. Leave the design to dry thoroughly before moving on to step 5.

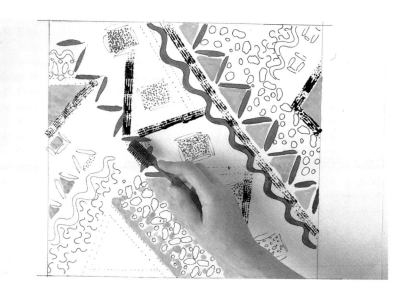

3

4 5

5. Take a piece of fabric slightly bigger than the design and secure it with masking tape to a flat surface. Choose a man-made fabric as the technique does not work on natural ones. Place the design face down on the fabric and attach it with masking tape. Set the iron on medium heat and iron the paper carefully from top to bottom. Take care not to move the paper during ironing.

6. Lift one corner of the paper to see if the design has transferred and to check colour density. If necessary continue ironing for a few more minutes.

6

142

7

8

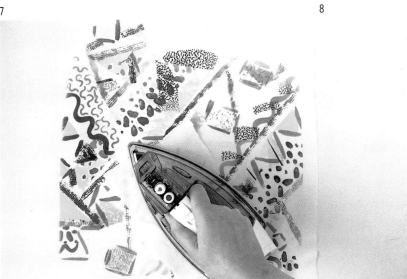

9

10

7. Once you are satisfied that the design has been transferred to the fabric, remove the paper. You can use the paper a second time, but the result will be paler. The fabric is permanent and needs no further fixing. If you want to make another print with the same colour density as the first, repaint the original paper design.

8. If you find that your final print contains gaps, or you feel you want to add more colour, you can iron individual textures on to the print. Paint them on to small pieces of paper and leave them to dry.

9. Iron the textures on to the fabric separately. Cover each one (or group if they are close together) with paper and iron until the design has transferred. Make sure you don't touch the fabric with the iron directly.

10. Remove all the textures. If you want paler textures iron the same ones again in different places. Or if you want darker ones, iron them again over your first attempts.

SCREEN PRINTING

The silk screen is a direct development of the Japanese stencil, in which fine silk mesh was originally used. The silk was stretched on to a rectangular wooden frame and the design, in stencil form, attached to the stretched surface of the fabric. Exactly the same principle applies now, and the only real difference is that the silk has been replaced with cheaper man-made fabrics, such as fine nylon and terylene.

Screen printing is widely used commercially for many different effects, from multicoloured, mass-produced fabrics, to more exclusive, hand-screen printed fabrics produced by small workshops and in limited quantities. Some of the processes and equipment used in screen printing are technical and expensive, and it would be impracticable to suggest that you could manage these at home. For example, many designs are reproduced photographically on to a screen and then used to produce great lengths of printed fabric. However, basic screen printing techniques are possible at home.

If you would like to use more complicated photographic images as a screen design, there are specialist studios and workshops that will transfer your image on to the screen, and this is not too expensive. Costs can rise, however, if your design has a number of colours, since each one requires a separate screen. To keep costs under control, limit yourself to a few colours or design a complicated one-colour pattern.

Other pieces of equipment needed are 5 cm (2 in) wide brown paper gumstrip, shellac varnish (or knotting) available from hardware stores, thin plain paper and an old sheet or curtain for testing your prints.

Testing is most important and,

tempting as it is to rush straight into your first project, you must check that your screen works correctly before trying it on fabric you plan to use for the finished article. It is also wise to invest in some cheap calico to place under the fabric to soak up paint seepage.

Mask the edges of your screen with gumstrip to prevent seepage around the print area itself. Cut four lengths to fit the inner edges. Fold them lengthwise and place half the gumstrip on the mesh and the other half on the frame. Push it down to make sure that it is firmly in place. Add another strip, overlapping the first for security. When they are thoroughly dry, coat the strips with shellac on both sides of the screen, making sure that none splashes on to the mesh. Place the frame on a flat surface, carefully balanced on four pencils to prevent it sticking in case the shellac is still tacky.

Wash and iron your calico and test fabric. Stretch the calico over the table, fasten it with masking tape and secure the test fabric on top.

Making your own equipment

The three basic pieces of equipment for screen printing are terylene or nylon, a frame and a squeegee. Art and craft shops as well as specialist silk screen suppliers will stock these, but you can easily make your own.

The frame itself is constructed from a 2.5 m (8 ft) length of 40 x 40 mm (1½ x 1½ in) planed softwood, but these sizes can be altered to suit your own purposes. Keep in mind that the inside dimensions of the frame should roughly correspond to the intended size of your designs and also allow a 10 cm (4 in) gap at the top and bottom for the excess dye to collect in.

To make a rectangular frame saw the

wood into two 78 cm (30 in) lengths and two 45 cm (18 in) lengths. Then apply woodworking glue to the ends of the individual lengths of wood to make the corners and hammer in corrugated fasteners, available from all hardware stores, to secure them. Finally, ensure that the frame is warp-free and lies absolutely flat on the table, and then sandpaper the frame smooth.

Once you have made the frame, select the fabric for the screen. This fabric should have a medium-gauge mesh to ensure the correct flow of paint. Terylene is probably the most suitable, but other alternatives are nylon and cotton organdie. Both produce good results but they are not as durable as terylene, and you will find that nylon also tends to lose a degree of tautness when wet.

First, cut a rectangle of fabric 10 cm (4 in) longer and wider than the outside dimensions of the frame. Then place it over the frame, ensuring that it drapes over each side equally. As you attach the fabric to the screen, you should turn the edges under 2.5 cm (1 in), since double fabric acts as a strong reinforcement when stretching. Use a heavy-duty staple gun (placing staples vertically for greater strength), tacks or drawing pins to secure the fabric to the frame. Start by stapling or pinning the fabric at the centre of the long sides and secure the double fabric turn, folding to the inside of the frame. Repeat this for the other longest side and then the shorter sides in turn. Then, starting from the centre points, staple or pin along to the corners. At the corners turn the loose fabric under neatly, and then attach it firmly.

The squeegee for use with the screen and frame needs to be at least

2.5 cm (1 in) shorter in length than the width of the inside frame measurement. This is to ensure that it will cover the screen area well and allow an amount of manoeuvrability. You can make your own squeegee, but it is easier to buy one. Squeegees with a pointed edge are more suitable for printing on cloth.

Preparation

Make sure you have a flat work surface that provides ample printing space. Pin out your fabric ensuring there are no puckers or wrinkles. Mark where you will be placing the screen with chalk to ensure even pattern repeats. Cover the table or worktop with a thick blanket or carpet underfelt (secured to the underside of your working surface with staples). Cover this with plastic or rubber sheeting and fasten it in place.

Print designs

Start with designs in a single colour. Paper stencils are simple to use and provide a good basis for later experimentation. Cut paper strips and attach them to the back of the screen to form a square area in which your design will sit. Chalk this square on to the test fabric, and then tear and cut paper strips and shapes and arrange them within the square.

Try different combinations until you are satisfied you have a well-balanced composition. Use overlapping and dissecting shapes or ragged edges contrasting with smooth, cut edges. When you have a design you are satisfied with, place the screen on the fabric so that the mesh surface covers the design. To ensure the frame is square, match up the chalk outline on the fabric with the taped square on the frame.

Printing process

It is most important that the screen is held steady, since any movement will distort and smudge your design and paint will seep into the wrong areas. Secure the frame with two G-clamps.

Place the squeegee centrally at the far end of the screen and then pour a line of fabric paint or ink into the gap between the squeegee and the frame wall. Holding the squeegee at both ends, place it behind the line of paint, tilt it slightly forward and drag it towards the opposite end of the screen, making sure that the paint is evenly distributed as you pull and that the pressure remains even. Repeat this in the opposite direction without adding any extra paint. Place the squeegee upright so that excess paint is captured behind it. Unclamp the frame (where necessary) and then, holding one end of the frame to steady it, lift it away gently from the opposite end, trying not to dislodge the fabric. The paper shapes will have adhered to the screen so you can easily repeat the pattern precisely.

For any subsequent designs in the same colour, it is best to run the squeegee over the screen on the test fabric to remove any trace of the former design.

As an alternative to paper shapes, striking results can be achieved with wax crayons, using a similar technique to brass rubbing. Place the screen over a textured surface or object and then rub it with a wax crayon. Mask out the non-printing areas with shellac and then remove the drawn areas with white spirit to leave your stencil.

Making a Profilm stencil

For a more professional and durable screen stencil, try experimenting with Profilm (available by the metre from art or craft stores). This is a transparent film with a peelable coating that allows you to cut away areas leaving the backing intact. The coating is melted on to the mesh with an iron.

First draw your design on to paper and tape it securely to your work surface. Then cut a piece of Profilm 5 cm (2 in) larger than your drawing and place it all round on your design, shiny side up. Secure it in place.

Next, cut out each section of the design to be printed with a scalpel or craft knife, and peel the film off, taking care to remove only the shiny coating and not the backing sheet. When this operation has been completed, wash the screen well in hot water to remove any grease.

Now cover your table with an old blanket and then add a sheet, making sure that there are no wrinkles. Place the Profilm, shiny side up, on the sheet and place the screen, with the mesh side down, on top of the Profilm, keeping it absolutely flat.

With an iron set to cool, iron the whole of the inside of the screen, first placing a sheet of paper over the design area to protect the Profilm. The coating will slowly melt away from its backing and adhere to the mesh. As this happens, the film becomes darker and when it is evenly dark, you should turn the screen over and carefully peel away the backing, leaving the film in place. If necessary, iron over any stubborn areas once more.

Now place strips of gumstrip over any gaps between the Profilm and the edges of the frame to prevent paint seeping through the mesh.

Finally, a special varnish treatment is required to protect a Profilm stencil from the water present in paints, dyes or inks. Brush the inside of the screen with polyurethane varnish, and rub the outside with white (mineral) spirit (the solvent for the polyurethane varnish). If you hold the screen up to the light you will be able to check that all of the varnish has been removed from the design area of the mesh. Reverse this process when the varnish is dry, using shellac on the outside of the screen and methylated spirit or denatured alcohol (the solvent for shellac) on the inside.

To remove the stencil, use paint stripper formulated for polyurethane and use methylated spirit for the shellac and Profilm. Use newspaper soaked in methylated spirit to soften the stencil and then rub it with a clean rag.

To print the same design more than once, for cushion covers or a repeat on a piece of fabric, for example, attach the frame with hinges to a piece of hardboard larger than the frame itself, and place registration marks on the board where the design will print each time. A piece of fabric can be wrapped round the hardboard just to make the surface more padded for printing. It will also help to absorb some of the fabric paint and prevent the hardboard becoming soaked. Lift up the screen, place the fabric inside the registration marks, lower the screen and print. Now lift the screen, remove the fabric and place it somewhere to dry before repeating the process. This is a quick and an easy way to produce a limited run of the same design in the same colour. Although if the screen is washed (with water) and dried another colour can be printed.

Equipment
Screens (various sizes)
Squeegees
Masking tape
Clean rags
Clean water
Paint brushes
Spoon
Varnish/brown tape
Knife
Binder
Printing ink (water-soluble)

1

2

1. You will need a silk screen, hinged to a board for easy registration, and a squeegee for pushing dye across the screen.

2. Use small amounts of concentrated fabric ink. Add the ink to a binder (ten parts to one). The binder acts as a thickening agent.

3. Sketch out your design ideas, keeping the motifs fairly simple. Draw out the shapes to actual size to make sure that they fit inside the screen area.

3

4

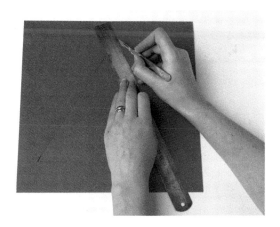

5

6

7

4. Try out different colour combinations, bearing in mind that colours can change when superimposed.

5. Cut out the triangle from a sheet of red paper, using a sharp knife and a metal ruler to ensure a straight edge.

6. Draw the cross shape in pencil on a sheet of pink paper and tear it out.

7. Draw a zig-zag shape on black paper and tear it out. Decide on your final design, then stick the shapes on a sheet of paper.

8. Make a separate paper stencil for each shape. The stencils must all be the same size as the back of the screen. The triangle must have at least 2 cm (¾ in) all around it when it is placed centrally on the screen. To make certain that each shape appears in the correct place on its individual stencil, trace off your original design. Then cut each stencil out.

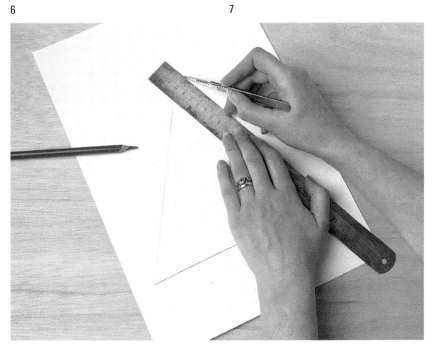

8

9

10

9. Draw registration marks on the screen so that the stencils can be positioned correctly for each printing. Then place the first stencil on the screen and secure it with masking tape.

10. Place a piece of crease-free fabric centrally on the board. Draw registration marks at each corner, on the board, so that you can replace the fabric in the same place for each printing. Secure the fabric with masking tape.

11. The silk screen is hinged and screwed to a board. The screws can be removed so that the screen is free from the board if you want to print a larger area of fabric. Also, the screen can be moved around a surface area if a repeat design is required.

12. Mix all the colours and remove any lumps and streaks. You need about one-third of a cup for the largest motif. Pour a line across one end of the closed screen, keeping the ink away from the edge of the motif.

13. Tilting the squeegee towards you, start pulling it smoothly and firmly across the closed screen.

11

12

13

14

15

16

17

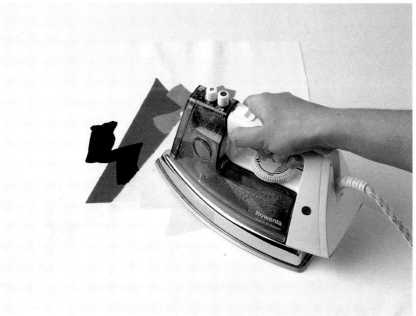

18

14. Continue pulling the squeegee across the screen, making sure that the ink has covered the whole motif. Then push the ink back up to the top of the screen again.

15. Scoop out any excess ink and remove the squeegee. Lift the screen and remove the fabric. Leave it to dry. Remove the stencil and throw it away. Wash the screen with water. The ink may stain the mesh, but this does not matter as long as there are no clogged areas. Leave the screen to dry.

16. Attach the second stencil to the back of the screen, using the registration marks to get the right position. Attach the fabric to the board again, using the registration marks for position. Repeat the printing process as before and wash the screen again.

17. Print the final motif. It is a good idea to print the darkest colour last. Leave the finished fabric to dry. Remove the stencil and then wash the screen in water.

18. When the fabric is dry, fix it by ironing for a few minutes. The fabric is now washable and dry-cleanable.

DYEING

Fabric dyes can transform and revive plain and printed fabrics, co-ordinate furnishing fabrics and give a new lease of life to a range of household linens.

Natural dyes are, generally, not available commercially. These types of dye are extracted from plants, but to achieve a strong colour density the plant material has to be collected in bulk, and some, such as nettles and certain barks, can be difficult to handle. Also with natural dyes, the actual colour is reliant on the time of year and at certain times some plants are simply not available for collection.

Chemical dyes have many advantages: they are readily available, results have been standardized and they are easy to use. There are a number of different types of chemical dyes on the market, and you must ensure you use one suitable for your fabric.

So before dyeing anything you need to know the composition of the fabric but, where furnishings are concerned, this can be difficult to ascertain. Even 'cotton' sheets are commonly a mixture of cotton and polyester, and dye will not take as strongly on a fabric that is a mix of man-made and natural fibres.

All natural fabrics take dye well, as do some polyesters, although the effect will be much paler. If you are not sure of your fabric's composition, dye a small test piece before proceeding with the whole article.

Types of dye

Broadly, there are two types of dye suitable for hand dyeing; one uses cold water, the other hot. Also available in the UK and Europe are hot water dyes specially formulated for use in automatic washing machines (any hot water dye can be used in non-automatics). In the United States, Australia and New Zealand, however, you cannot successfully dye fabric in a washing machine. Machines in these countries take in too much water and results tend to be very pale and washed out.

Cold water dyes

These are suitable only for natural fabrics. The colours are very stable if fixed in the appropriate way, and they will withstand frequent washing. Cold water dyes are ideal for bed-linen, towels, curtains, tablecloths and wool, although when used on wool colours will be paler.

When buying the dye, always check the manufacturer's instructions to ensure you have the right fixing ingredients – salt, vinegar or a special fix for that particular dye. Again, read the instructions and make sure you have sufficient dye for the weight of fabric to be treated.

Try to keep the fabric moving continually to avoid patchy results. Large articles can be dyed in a non-automatic washing machine if you have a machine with a cold wash setting. Cold water dyes should wash out of any vessel used with no problem. If, however, there is a stain left behind, use detergent and a small amount of bleach to remove it.

Hot water dyes

Traditionally, hot water dyes for hand dyeing require boiling water, but newly formulated products just need hot tap water, making them far more convenient to use.

Before dyeing new fabrics, make sure you first remove any fabric finish or dressing or the dye will not take properly. For hand dyeing you will need a suitably sized heat-proof container, such as an old pan or metal bucket and, as with cold water dyeing, you will have to keep the fabric moving throughout the process.

For the most successful results with hot water dyes, it is best to use a washing machine. Make sure you do not overload the machine with too much fabric or use too little dye, and the dye will take better if the fabric is clean and wet before it is put in the machine. To clean the machine afterwards, run it empty through a wash cycle.

Dyeing different fabrics

It is not possible to dye fabric a lighter colour. There are products available, however, designed to remove stains and colour so the fabric can be redyed. Bear in mind that fabric looks a few shades darker when wet, so don't be impatient to remove it from the dye bath too soon.

Coloured fabrics can be dyed, but the colour change will depend on the background colour (see the chart opposite). To avoid this, strip out the original colour beforehand. Unlike paint, dyes are transparent and will not obliterate the colour underneath.

Bear in mind that colours will look different on different types of fabric, and the same colour used to dye a piece of silk, for example, will look different if used to dye a piece of towelling or some other textured fabric. Printed, multi-coloured fabrics can also be dyed, but look at all the colours carefully and try to gauge the likely colour reactions.

Equipment
Old bucket or rustproof vessel
Rubber gloves
Jar
Stick (to move article around in dye)

AGEING FABRIC

A quick and effective way to create an aged look on fabrics is to soak them in cold tea. A white or pale fabric will take on a yellowed hue when treated in this way. Delicate laces, crochet and broderie anglaise are particularly suited to this technique, and it also works well on modern furnishing braids by subduing bright colours. Alternatively, place fabrics in a small amount of blue non-permanent ink diluted with water, then hang out to dry. The colour will gradually fade out, especially when exposed to bright sunlight.

COLOUR CHANGES WITH DYES

FABRIC	DYE	RESULT
BLUE	YELLOW	GREEN
RED	BLUE	PURPLE
RED	GREEN	KHAKI
PURPLE	RED	BROWN
YELLOW	RED	ORANGE
YELLOW	PINK	PEACH
PINK	BLUE	LILAC

CHILDREN'S TECHNIQUES

An interesting technique for children to try is transfer inks and crayons (see page 140). Drawing and painting with these on paper and then transferring the drawings on to fabric by ironing is always fascinating to watch under supervision.

Shop-bought stencils of letters and numbers are ideal for children to use, especially if the stencils are painted on to the fabric using special felt-tip pens. These have two nib sizes and they do not create any messy smudges; nor do the colours bleed. Names and numbers can be easily and perfectly stencilled on to fabric, but for large areas of stencilling use paint (see page 153). Children can use the felt-tips directly on fabric in just the same way as they would draw with ordinary pens on paper.

Heat-expanding paints (see page 154) also need an iron to complete the process. Use the paint straight from the tube directly on to the fabric. When the paint is perfectly dry, turn the fabric pattern-side down and iron the back for a few minutes. Turn the fabric pattern-side up and see how the surface has risen like rubber.

Children might find searching for objects to print with, and then deciding which ones would work best, just as enjoyable as the actual printing process. Anything with a textured surface can be used to print with, or it could be used as a reverse stencil. An old metal grid (cleaned), for example, could be laid across the fabric and painted or sprayed over. When removed, the shape of the grid is left as the background colour. This can be very effective with any interesting shape, but always wait until the paint is completely dry before removing the object.

String and rope are also very versatile and, with a little imagination, exciting fabric designs can be created with them. Stiff rope is excellent because it can be moulded into different shapes. To print these successfully, first glue the rope shape to a block of wood. Paint over the rope's surface and press it down on to the fabric (see page 138).

A technique all children master at school is printing with fruit, vegetables, leaves and feathers. This method can just as easily be used on fabric as on paper, and it can produce a more sophisticated design than you first might think.

To print successfully on fabric using these objects, bear in mind two important points: first, use a sharp knife for cutting so that you have a smooth flat surface to press on to the fabric; second, before printing leave the cut fruit or vegetables for half an hour to allow any excess moisture to dry out – otherwise colours may bleed.

Some of these techniques are easier than others, some give more sophisticated results and some are more fun to do. Whenever children are involved, however, supervision and help will be required at some stage. Always experiment and practise on scraps of fabric – don't let the first attempt be on new fabrics or an expensive duvet cover.

FABRIC AND PAINT GUIDE

Natural fabrics such as silk, wool and cotton are the most suitable for textile painting and printing, although fabric paints do take to most kinds of cloth, including man-made ones. Because the feel of natural fabrics is so much more luxurious it is best, where possible, to use them. Silk is a luxury fabric but it is, nowadays, quite inexpensive to buy. A cheap jap type would be suitable when trying out silk paints.

Most people tend to choose natural fabrics for soft furnishings, anything from an inexpensive calico to an elaborate silk brocade. Some paints, though, will only work on man-made cloth: if used on natural fabrics they tend to be very pale and not permanent. However, there are many man-made types that imitate natural fabrics very well. For a beginner, it is always advisable to use a cheap fabric, or something you already have, such as old sheeting, until you have mastered a few of the basic techniques.

There are many types of silks and cottons, as well as man-made fabrics, and it may be a good idea to look round a few department stores, checking on the different qualities before deciding. Silk, for example, comes in a variety of textures, from a fine, smooth, sheer cloth to a heavy, rough, textured one, which many would find difficult to recognize as silk (see page 27). Cotton can be smooth and soft too, like cotton lawn, or a rough, natural-coloured canvas (see page 26). Man-made textiles tend to imitate both these categories, and a sheer type might be suitable for draping at windows. Although the look and feel of natural fabrics is far more enticing than man-made ones, they need more care in cleaning and they do tend to crease more easily.

All fabrics need to be washed or dry-cleaned before use in order to remove any manufacturer's finish or dressing. If not, the fabric paint will not adhere to the surface very well and would probably wash out. If the fabric is old, make sure it is dry, clean and crease-free before you start to paint.

NATURAL FABRICS

Cottons

Calico This is a mediumweight fabric that often has a matte finish in its natural state. When untreated, it is a creamy colour with brown flecks. It can be found in quite a range of widths, it is very cheap and it would be ideal for a beginner to practise on.

Canvas A heavy fabric, unbleached. It is often used as a theatrical backdrop and by artists for painting on, therefore it comes in very generous widths. Canvas can be used successfully as a furnishing fabric, and it works particularly well when thrown over a sofa or chair or when draped at windows.

Chintz This sometimes has a glossy finish and is also known as glazed cotton. It is usually printed with traditional motifs, such as birds and flowers.

Damask This is an ancient type of fabric weave, first executed in silk in Damascus. It is now woven in cotton and is available in many weights. It is commonly used for table-linen.

Holland A plain-weave fabric, usually made of cotton. It is very hard wearing and it is commonly used, when stiffened, for roller-blinds.

Lace An open-work fabric in a variety of constructions. Traditionally made of linen, it is now more commonly made in cotton, nylon or viscose. The more decorative pieces of lace can look stunning at a window with parts of the pattern picked out in soft painted colours.

Lawn A lightweight cotton fabric, soft and fresh looking. It does crease and so it is probably more suited to dressmaking, but it looks attractive when used on cushions or in bedrooms.

Organdie This crisp cotton fabric is almost sheer and very lightweight. It is suitable for use at windows.

Percale This is a close-weave cotton similar to poplin, with a smooth, firm surface. It cleans and wears well and is excellent for sheets and duvet covers.

Poplin A hard-wearing, mediumweight fabric. It is traditionally made of cotton and it has a slight sheen. It tends to crease unless mixed with polyester.

Sateen This weave has a sheen on the right side. It is quite a heavy fabric and is used for loose covers and curtains.

Voile A soft, plain-weave fabric made of fine yarns. It is very flimsy, but it is ideal for draping at windows.

Silks

Crepe de chine A luxurious fabric, very soft and flowing, and with a slight sheen. It folds and hangs beautifully. The cheaper man-made polyester crepe de chine is a good copy. It washes well but somehow does not have the same look or feel.

Jap silk A very fine, smooth silk, and one of the cheapest. It is often used as a lining, but it is particularly suitable for dyeing and painting.

Noil A fabric with quite a rough but very attractive appearance. Not at first glance recognizable as silk, it has dark cream flecks woven into the lighter cream background.

Shantung A slubbed silk yarn with a texture and a slightly knobbly appearance. It is very attractive.

Tussah Also known as wild silk. This is quite a thick fabric, almost like hessian in appearance. The yarn has an uneven slub, which gives it a rough texture.

Twill A weave with a diagonal line on the right side of the fabric. It is usually woven in silk, but it can be made of any natural or man-made fibre.

Other natural fabrics

Linen A strong yarn made from flax. The yarn can be used for all types of weaves and weights and it is suitable for garments and household furnishings. It is expensive, however, and it creases very badly, but it can look stunning if used in an appropriate setting.

Velvet This is a pile cloth made of silk, cotton or a man-made fibre. It can be made with a crushed effect. It takes dye extremely well if made of natural fibres, and it can be used with some fabric paints. Use silk paints on silk velvet.

Wool Fabrics made from wool are warm and easy to manipulate. Wool comes in many guises, from fine wool crepe to thick woollen blankets, suitable as throwovers. Fine wools can be dyed or painted, but the thicker, more textured, tweedy wools are too thick, and the surface too fuzzy, to paint on successfully.

MAN-MADE FABRICS

Nylon A sheer fabric used for curtains and drapes. It handles well and is quite hard wearing.

Polyester This material takes on various guises and it can successfully imitate many silks, although the feel is not quite as luxurious. Polyester washes well, is hard wearing and does not crease easily. It is often mixed with other fabric – polyester-cotton is a widely used combination.

Ultrasuede This is a soft synthetic suede. Although expensive, it looks and feels like the real thing. It is much easier to handle, however, and can be machine washed. Unlike genuine suede, which is sold by the skin, ultrasuede is bought by the metre. This is a good material for painting, particularly transfer printing (see page 140).

FABRIC PAINT

Readily available in small pots or large 1 litre (approximately 1¾ pt) bottles, the standard fabric paints can be used on all silks, cottons and man-made fabrics. The colour range is huge, all the colours are intermixable and they can be diluted in water. Paints are available in four different finishes – pearlized, fluorescent, transparent and opaque – and they will react differently depending on the weight and nature of the fabric used. Some fabric paints, such as the pearlized types, sit on the cloth. This also happens if quite a lot of white is mixed with a colour.

Obviously, mixing white with a colour produces a pastel tone. If this is the desired colour, always add colour to white in small amounts. The fabric paints are quite concentrated, so don't mix them the other way round: the chances are the colour will not be pale enough and this could mean a lot of waste. A pastel colour will sit on the fabric, so it is acceptable to use it on a fabric with a dark background.

Other paints, such as transparent or silk fabric paints, sink into the fabric and the resulting colour will be very muddy. Therefore, it is advisable to use a fabric that has a pale background with these types of paint.

The amount of fabric paint you use will depend on the technique and the coverage required. Spattering, for example, uses up quite a lot of paint, while sponging and stencilling spread out the paint thinly and are quite economical. Obviously you do not have to buy every colour you will need: we all know blue and yellow make green, therefore a pot of green is unnecessary. Black and white are always useful for darkening or lightening other colours.

Mix colours by pouring small amounts on to an old saucer. If the colour is acceptable then mix more. Make sure you have enough to work with without mixing another batch, as you may not be able to hit on an exact colour match. If you have any paint left over, store it in a clean, airtight jar. Fabric paints have quite a long life.

The consistency of the paint will depend on the technique being used. Too thin, and it will bleed when painted on to the fabric; too thick, and it will leave the fabric stiff. Always leave the fabric paint to dry before painting a second coat. The fabric should be kept flat until the design is finished and completely dry.

Information on fixing (making permanent) all commercial fabric paints is given on page 155.

SPECIAL PAINTS

Fabric pens

These pens look and work like ordinary felt tips, but they are specially designed for drawing on to fabrics. Most types of fabric are suitable. The felt tip is tapered to produce both thick and thin lines, although a fine tip is also available. The pens can be refilled and tips replaced. When used in conjunction with ordinary fabric paints, it would be difficult to tell the difference between the colour effects.

Fabric pens are easy to use and they are particularly useful when painting outlines or intricate areas of pattern. A total beginner may prefer fabric pens to start with since they are easier to control, particularly when designing 'doodles or scribbles' on fabric. Try out the pens first on scraps of cloth just to get the feel of how they work and to gain some idea of the surfaces that are most receptive. Always use pale fabrics, since the pens will not show up on dark ones. If the fabric is quite taut the pens will be easier to use. They can also be used with any other type of fabric paint in the same design.

Heat-expanding paint

This is an opaque paint in a tube that can be used on any fabric, including leather and suede. Because of its rubber-like texture, though, it is not advisable for use on silk. The most appropriate use of this paint is for creating abstract designs on T-shirts. This type of paint is not recommended for fabrics that are washed frequently.

The paint is not difficult to use, but a bit of practice may be necessary to control the nozzle when drawing with it straight from the tube. For a linear design, squeeze the paint from the tube very gently on to the fabric, applying more pressure for a thicker line. For larger areas, it can be applied to the fabric with a brush. When the paint is dry, use a medium-hot iron on the reverse side. Then turn the fabric over and you will find that the heat has expanded the paint, which now has the appearance of a raised rubber-like substance. Fabrics treated with this paint

can be washed carefully by hand.

Fabric crayons

These have the same appearance on fabric as they do on paper. Use the crayons directly on fabric, being careful not to smudge them. It is important to protect your iron from staining by covering the finished crayon design with a clean piece of fabric before applying heat. The crayons can be used on all man-made and natural fabrics and in conjunction with any of the paints and pens. The crayons are particularly suitable for children attempting to decorate fabric, although supervision is necessary when it comes to fixing.

Silk paints

As the name suggests, these are made specially for silk. They are transparent and have a vibrant, translucent quality. The colours may be thinned with water and they are intermixable. Traditional professional silk paints are just as easy to use as the commercial types designed for amateurs, but they do need to be steam fixed. Most commercial silk paints require no more than ironing, although some manufacturers advise rinsing the painted fabric in a solution of water and vinegar – 1 teaspoon of vinegar/570 ml (1 pt) of water – to help the silk regain its original softness after it has been fixed.

Because of the variation in the treatment of these paints, it is always vital to read the instructions carefully. The paints work directly on to silk, and often a diffusing agent should be mixed with the paint. The diffusing agent is a liquid that slows down the drying time of the paint. It is used to prevent hard lines appearing when covering large, flat areas of fabric or when colours need to merge gradually. Silk paints can be used with a spray diffuser (see page 129).

Transfer paints

These are for use on man-made fabrics only. They can be used on fabrics that are mixtures, such as polyester cotton, but the effect is rather dull, since colours tend to be too pale. These paints can be bought individually in small pots or sets of eight or ten, or more ambitious litre (1¾ pt) bottles are available. All the colours are intermixable and can be diluted with water to create paler tones, but they should not be mixed with other fabric paints. Once printed, however, other fabric paints can be used in the same design to create a different effect or to give more depth to the design.

Before the paints are transferred on to the fabric by heat the colours are very dull and murky in appearance. But once on the fabric they appear brilliant, some almost fluorescent. Therefore, it is quite important to test each colour before using it. This can be achieved easily by painting a small blob of each colour on a piece of thin paper. Leave it to dry and then turn it reverse side up on a small piece of man-made fabric, such as polyester. With the iron on the medium-hot setting, iron it for a few minutes, checking the colour density before removing the iron. You will be able to see the contrast to the dull painted paper and the vivid hues on the fabric.

Transfer crayons

These crayons come in small packets, just like conventional crayons, and you use them in much the same way. Like transfer paints, they appear very dull on paper but they take on a vivid appearance when transferred by heat on to man-made fabric. Again, it is vital to test the colours before use. New colours and textures can be created by drawing one colour on top of another.

Protect your iron when transferring the designs, since the wax from the crayons, once softened, can be messy.

Screen printing inks

Most fabric paints can be used for screen printing, but it is best to use a thickening agent or binder to extend their coverage. However, if you plan on being more ambitious, it may be worth investigating industrial inks and paints, which are available in small quantities. These inks are a lot more concentrated than conventional fabric paints and must be used with a binder – only a drop of ink need be added to the binder to produce an intense colour.

The same rules governing the use of fabric paints apply here: always add colour to binder or white. It is easy to add too much colour and then very difficult to make that colour paler again. Usually you will have to start all over and store the unsuitable colour for use at a later date.

Screen printing inks are suitable for any type of fabric. They can be diluted with water and the screen comes clean with ordinary water. The ink is fixed in the same way as fabric paints.

Spray paints

Paint in cans formulated for use on autos can be used on some fabrics. However, this paint has two disadvantages for fabric decorators: it isn't washable and it stiffens the fabric. Therefore it is best used for roller blinds, deckchairs, floorcloths and similar applications. Coverage should be light and even. This takes a little practice, so test on scrap fabric first. To prevent spray drifting outside the perimeters of your design, use low-tack masking tape or a piece of cardboard as a guard. As you gain expertise, you will be able to control the concentration of colour in different areas. This skill can be used to indicate light (with a sparse distribution of pigment) and shade (with a heavier distribution of colour)

If the spray nozzle becomes blocked during use, clear it with a pin and wipe over the nozzle head with acetone.

Auto spray paints are particularly effective when used with stencils (see page 132).

Professional colours

These special dyes and paints are more economical for large pieces. However, they are not readily available in the shops, so you will have to contact a specialist supplier (see page 157). Some types need steam fixing, and therefore aren't suitable for amateur use.

Acrylic paints

Available as a quick-drying type, specially formulated for stencilling, or a slower-drying artist's version. Acrylics are only suitable for fabrics that can't be washed or dry-cleaned – roller blinds or matting, for example.

FIXING

With the exception of spray paints and some silk paints, all fabric paints are made permanent (fixed) using the same technique. First, leave the fabric flat until it is completely dry. Then, cover it with a clean piece of cloth and iron it with a medium-hot iron for a few minutes. Protect the ironing board with old, clean sheeting. The fabric will now be washable and dry-cleanable.

CLEANING INSTRUCTIONS

Always consult the manufacturer's instructions before washing. In general, unless decorated with auto spray paints, hand painted or printed fabrics can be washed in a machine or by hand. Use a mild detergent and warm water.

For non-washable items like screens, close covers and blinds dirt can be kept at bay by vacuuming them regularly, with the nozzle held about an inch above the fabric.

Dyed fabrics can also be washed in a machine or by hand. However, dyed articles should be washed separately from undyed ones as the colour may bleed into the rest of the wash.

USEFUL ADDRESSES

To see hand painted or printed fabrics:

Contemporary Textiles Gallery,
10 Golden Square, Soho,
London W1.
Gallery showing hand printed and painted textiles

Design Centre,
28 Haymarket, London SW1.
Exhibition centre/Design index

Crafts Council,
8 Waterloo Place, London SW1.
Exhibitions/Design index

Liberty Department Store,
210-220 Regent Street, London W1.
One-offs, hand painted fabrics

Timney-Fowler,
388 Kings Road, London SW3
Hand printed fabrics

Celia Birtwell,
71 Westbourne Park Road,
London W2.
Hand printed fabrics

Collier Campbell,
63 Old Town, London SW4.
Printed fabrics

Bentley & Spens, Studio 25,
90 Lots Road, London SW10

Mary Fox Linton,
249 Fulham Road, London SW3.
Hand painted fabrics

Reputation, 186 Kensington Park Road, London W11.
Hand painted/printed fabrics

Equipment suppliers

Macullogh & Wallis Ltd,
25 Dering Street, London W1.
Silk/cotton specialist

George Weill
Riding House Street, London W1.
Silk/cotton specialist, silk dye/transfer paints

C.I. Davis & Co,
94-96 Seymour Place, London W1.
Silk specialists

Ian Mankin,
109 Regents Park Road, London NW1
Silks and cottons

Russell & Chapple,
23 Monmouth Street,
London WC2.

Cowling and Wilcox,
26-28 Broadwick Street,
London W1.
Paints and dyes

Rowney,
12 Percy Street, London W1.
Paints and dyes

Dryad Craft Centre,
Kensington High Street, London W8.
Kits, dyes and paints

Durham Chemicals,
55-57 Glengall Road, London SE15.
Dyes and inks

Bolloms,
107-115 Long Acre, London WC2.
Paints and dyes

Plotons,
273 Archway Road,
London N6.
Paints and dyes

Paperchase Products Ltd.
213 Tottenham Court Road, London W1.
Stencil kits

Dylon International Ltd.,
Worsley Bridge Road,
Lower Sydenham, London SE26.
Dyes, information on home dyeing

Artemis Products,
684 Mitcham Road, Croydon CR9 3AB.
Dyes and equipment

Carolyn Warrender,
91-93 Lower Sloane Street,
London SW1.
Stencil equipment

Winsor and Newton,
51 Rathbone Place, London W1.
Paints, dyes, silk screen kits

Eurostudio Ltd, Unit 4, Southdown Industrial Estate, Southdown Road,
Harpenden, Herts AL5 1PW
Stencil kits

Stencil-itis, P.O. Box 30,
Rickmansworth, Herts.
Stencilling products

INDEX

INDEX

ACKNOWLEDGEMENTS

Addresses of Textile Designers

Joanna Beale
7 Healey Wood Bottom
Rastrick
Brighouse
West Yorkshire HD6 1HU

Penny Beard
1st Floor
28-30 Coronet Street
London NI 6HD

Cressida Bell
32 Fortescue Avenue
London E8 3QB

The Bleach Boys
113 Redbridge Gardens
Southampton Way Estate
London SE5 7HB

Blind Alley
7 The Square
Praze-An-Beeble
Cornwall TR14 0JR

Celia Birtwell
71 Westbourne Park Road
London W2 5QH

Gabrielle Bolton
128 Riverview Gardens
London SW13 9RA

Paul Burgess
73 Pascoe Road
London SE13 5JE

Yvonne Chambers
Studio 228
Highbury Workshops
22 Highbury Grove
London N5 2EA

Ann Chiswell Designs
34 Queens Drive
London W3 0HA

Sarah Collins
Home Farm
Delaport
Wheathampstead
Hertfordshire AL4 8RQ

Lucy Clive Textiles
9 Ellesmere Road
London W4 3DU

Ros Cross
c/o
Aspects of Applied Art
109 Highbury Hill
London N5 1TA

Annie Doherty
The Craft Centre
Hungerford Arches
Southbank
London SE1

Dragons of Walton Street
23 Walton Street
London SW3 2HX

Julia Fieldwick
The Old House
Wissenden
Bethesden
Ashford, Kent

Frannie
Studio 23
Ransomes Dock
35-37 Parkgate Road
London SWII 0PL

Gallery of Antique Furniture and Decoration
2 Church Street
London NW8 8ED

Sally Guy
4 Somerville Road
Stamford
Lincolnshire
PE9 1BW

Nicola Henley
"The Gazebo"
Estcourt House
72 Park Road
Stapleton
Bristol BS16 1AU

Maison Design
917-919 Fulham Road
London SW6 5HU

Miroslava
3 Avon Road
London SE4 1QQ

Helen Napper
5 Castle Hill
Orford
Suffolk

Pazuki Prints
2 Beverley Gardens
London SW13 0LZ

Jo Pui Design Partnership
10 Mannville Terrace
Bradford
Yorkshire BD7 1AB

Carolyn Quartermaine
72 Philbeach Gardens
London SW5 9EY

Reputation
186 Kensington Park Road
London W11 2ES

Sara Robbins
45-46 Charlotte Road
London EC2 2A 3PD

Annie Sherburne
Unit 15
30 Sumner Road
London SE15 6LA

The Sleeping Company
65 Wigmore Street
London W1H 9LG

ACKNOWLEDGEMENTS

Laura Stirling
26 Inchmurrin Drive
Wardneuk
Kilmarnock KA3 2JD
Scotland

Jasia Szerszynska
144 Haberdasher Street
London NI 6EJ

Malcolm Temple
Agent: Patricia Higgins
5 Stronsa Road
London W12 9LB

Anna Tilson
23 Dalby Road
London SW18 1AW

Timney-Fowler Ltd.
388 Kings Road
London SW3 5UZ

Tissunique Ltd.
10 Princes Street
Hanover Square
London W1R 7RD

Sian Tucker
346 Old Street
London EC1V 9NQ

Jon Lys Turner
29 Curtain Road
London EC2A 3BX

K Virgils
c/o Aspects of Applied Art
109 Highbury Hill
London N5 1TA

Paul Wearing
The Bureaux
65 Farringdon Road
London EC1M 3JB

Fanny Wilder
22 Iliffe Yard
Crampton Street
London SE17 3QA

Althea Wilson
43 Burnaby Street
London SW10 0PW

Alison Wootten
34-36 Seel Street
Liverpool L1 4BE

Props suppliers

Rupert Cavendish
610 Kings Road
London SW6

Dragons of Walton Street
23 Walton Street
London SW3

Echo Prop Hire
514 Fulham Road
London SW6

The Kilim Warehouse
28A Pickets Street
London SW12

Osborne & Little
304 Kings Road
London SW3

Indiaworks
107A Pimlico Road
London SW1

Valerie Wade
89 Ebury Street
London SW1

Juliet Dunn
126 Long Acre
London WC2

Mary Fox Linton
249 Fulham Road
London SW3

The author and publishers would like to thank the following people and companies for their kind contribution to this book:

For supplying fabric for the front jacket photograph: Cressida Bell, Reputation and Tissunique Ltd.

For supplying fabric for the back jacket photograph: Timney-Fowler Ltd.

For supplying props for special photography:

Rupert Cavendish, Dragons of Walton Street, Echo Prop Hire, The Kilim Warehouse, Osborne & Little, Indiaworks, Valerie Wade, Timney-Fowler Ltd., Juliet Dunn, Mary Fox Linton.

For allowing us to photograph her home: Pam Loveday.

For supplying materials for special photography: Dylon Ltd, Artemis Ltd.

The publishers would like to thank the following for their permission to reproduce the photographs in this book:

p7 Zandra Rhodes/Robyn Beeche; p8 Victoria & Albert Museum, London; p9 Bridgeman Art Library; p10,11 and 13 V & A; p14 Bridgeman Art Library; p15 above Gallery of Antique Furniture and Decoration, below and p16 Design Council; p19 and 20 V & A; p21 Design Council; p22 Aspects of Applied Art/Ros Cross; p37 right Camera Press Ltd/IMS; p38 Cressida Bell; p40 Patrica Higgins; p46 right photo Liesa Siegelmann; p47 photo Robyn Beeche; p58 Althea Wilson; p67 right Elizabeth Whiting and Associates; p70 photo Brian Rybolt; p71 Alison Wootten; p76 and 79 Syndication International; p80 World of Interiors/Bill Batten; p84 National Magazine Company; p85 photo Charlie Wilder; p86 The Sleeping Company/Jon Lys Turner; p86 The Sleeping Company; p89 Syndication International; p90 Maison de Marie-Claire/ Bouchet; p97 Syndication International; p100 Camera Press ltd; p101 Syndication International; p102 Camera Press Ltd; p104 Maison de Marie-Claire; p105 Camera Press Ltd; p107 Maison de Marie-Claire; p108 Nicola Henley; p110 Aspects of Applied Art; p111 below and 113 Crafts Council; p117 Dragons of Walton Street; p123 Maison; p124 Penny Beard

Every effort has been made to trace the copyright holders of photographs, and we apologise in advance for any unintentional omissions and would be pleased to insert the appropriate acknowledgement in any subsequent edition of this publication.